What Others Are Saying

Susan Phillips shares her professional approach to home staging in easy-to-follow steps, allowing readers to put her vast experience into immediate practice. If you're selling your home, this is a must-read. In fact, even if you're not selling just yet, "The Seductive Power of Home Staging" can help you bring out your home's best assets.

Kimberley Seldon, Kimberley Seldon Design Group, Toronto, Canada
www.kimberleyseldon.com

This is brilliant. Finally, a book written by a real person, with real experience. It is one thing to do what you've been taught in school, and completely another to present what you've lived, observed, tried and built on – with a proven track record for success. Two things that stood out for me: it is not just a matter of shoving furniture around, or sterilizing the place. As a former realtor I can absolutely support what is written. A well-staged home is a SOLD home – not just any staging, but Staging Susan's Way - homes that I would want to live in.

Angela Sutcliffe, Sutcliffe Consulting, Ottawa, Canada
www.angelasutcliffe.com

I am not a book reader! But when I picked up Susan's book I read it in one weekend. It was entertainingly written while teaching me the steps necessary to get the most value when selling my house with the least amount of stress. I enjoyed it so much that I am purchasing copies to give my two girls who will likely be selling their houses in the near future. From a financial planning perspective, the book illustrates the steps necessary to get the highest return on the biggest investment most of us ever make. Happy reading.

Elsie Campbell, Certified Decorative Artist, Carlton Place, Canada
www.EM-Bellish.com

To all prospective home-sellers: I am like you in that I thought my home would sell as-is. My wife and I had lived in it making many improvements along the way and thought it was beautiful. But it wasn't selling. We couldn't figure out why. Having done all the things we thought would make it more presentable, like getting rid of clutter, didn't help.

Like you, I was concerned about what I should do, wondering if anyone could really help.

Well, now I know. Susan Phillips of Spotlight on Decor became our 'Stage Coach' - she advised us on how to stage our home for better presentation. Getting rid of clutter wasn't enough. Reorganizing the furniture to make the place look bigger (and it did!), buying a few tasteful artifacts that suited certain specific show-spots and repainting a few walls gave the house a bright new look.

Best of all it was easier to prepare for a showing and thereby relieved a load of stress, just like it will do for you! The house sold in a declining market at the price we expected. We were thrilled. I strongly recommend using Susan's expertise to assist you in staging your home for resale. Her impeccable taste and objective perspective made our lives much easier.

Mike Gillissie, C.R.S.P., R.O.H.T., ROSE Environmental Services
Carleton Place, Ontario, www.rosenv.com

As a financial advisor, when a client is selling their house I can't think of a better return on investment than following the staging advice in Susan's book!

Judith Cane, Antara Financial Group, Ottawa, Canada
www.antarafinancial.com

A very informative, yet relaxing read. As well, the author paints a vivid picture about her personal experiences making the book even more enjoyable."

Darlene Hall-Barratt, Dressing Rooms,
www.dressingrooms.ca

Our home sold for over the listing price in 13 days after being prepared for re-sale with the help of Susan Phillips at Spotlight on Decor. The effort that was put in to update the flooring, wall colour, and accessories paid off. I was really happy with how everything looked. Thanks for all your help!

Jennifer MacLean. Nepean, Ontario Canada

The Seductive Power of Home Staging:

A Seven-Step System for a Fast and Profitable Sale

Susan Victoria Phillips

Ottawa, Ontario Canada

This edition published by
Dog Ear Publishing
4010 W. 86th Street, Ste H
Indianapolis, IN 46268

www.dogearpublishing.net

ISBN: 978-159858-931-3
Library of Congress Control Number: Applied For
This book is printed on acid-free paper.

Printed in the United States of America

For my husband Gerry who has shown love and patience while I realize my dream.

You see things; and you say, 'Why?'
But I dream things that never were; and I say,
'Why not?'

~ George Bernard Shaw

Contents

Contents

About the Author

Susan Victoria Phillips became interested in design at a very early age. "It all began", she recalls, "when I watched my mother design fabulous ball gowns for Queen Elizabeth's court in London, England". The coordination of colour, texture, harmony and form has been an ongoing passion ever since.

Today, Susan is a Certified Interior Designer and a Home Staging Consultant, owner of Spotlight on Décor. In her spare time her passion in design extends to the theatre where she demonstrates her expertise as a Set Designer. Her most notable theatrical accomplishment was creating the stage design for the Dalai Lama's visit to Ottawa in 2007.

"Choosing the design for a theatrical performance, whether it's for Shakespeare or the Dalai Lama, and selecting the decor for a client's home, follows similar principles", Susan explains. "Reading a script and learning how the characters interact is much the same as learning how my clients use their space, the mood they wish to convey and in all cases how to bring it all together in harmony".

Susan can also be found working with the television hosts on CBC and Roger's television presenting the latest decorating trends and demonstrating quick and easy do-it-yourself projects for the homeowner.

As an Approved Education Provider for the Real Estate Council of Ontario and the Canadian Association for Accredited Mortgage Professionals, Susan delivers training courses in Home Staging in cities across the country. She holds a Diploma in Interior Design with an Award of Merit and is an active member of the Canadian Decorator's Association.

Susan brings to her clients a diverse background and a unique blend of experiences.

Foreword

I was approached by Susan Phillips to read a draft of her new book, *The Seductive Power of Home Staging: A Seven-Step System for a Fast and Profitable Sale* and provide her with my professional opinion of it. While I was honoured by having been asked, it was my busiest time of year and I was somewhat hesitant to commit due to time constraints. Once I got started however, I found Susan's book to be extremely enjoyable and hard to put down. I read it from cover to cover with genuine interest throughout.

What a great book and excellent approach to staging a home!

As a full time professional home inspector since 1980 and having completed over 17,000 residential home inspections, I've seen the good, the bad and the ugly when it comes to resale properties. Many of the sellers could have benefited greatly from reading this book had it been available.

Susan's no nonsense approach to home staging is a straightforward, honest and refreshing as opposed to many "Stagers" who do their best to sterilize a home and camouflage it's defects, which is often referred to as "white-washing" a home. Susan's staging suggestions, explain how to stage your home properly and avoid the pitfalls of home staging. I see a lot of home sales fall through for reasons that are not expensive or difficult to resolve. If the people selling these homes had read Susan's book and followed her suggestions, which includes having a pre-listing home inspection, to determine the major "red flags" in advance, the outcome could have been vastly different.

Susan's suggestion of determining deficiencies prior to listing your home for sale is "bang on" in my opinion for several reasons. Firstly, there is a very good chance that your purchasers will insist on having a home inspection of their own. Many times the pre-purchase inspection will reveal very serious and costly issues which may immediately kill a deal. Did the owners know about these serious issues? Often they don't. Other times however, the deal killer may involve a deficiency or condition that was easy and inexpensive to fix and yet the homeowner never bothered. Why gamble or try to second guess if there are issues with your home? Obtain an unbiased opinion from your home inspector and home stager. If you know in advance, your task of staging and selling your home should be much easier.

Foreword

It's amazing how many home offers fall through repeatedly after several home inspections and yet the vendors never bother to find out why. If they had followed Susan's advice and conducted a pre-listing inspection, they would have known in advance the issues with their home and the general cost to repair or replace deficient items. Susan's 'Chapter 5, Step 1 - Red Flags' reflects what I encounter on a daily basis. Her advice on these possible "deal busters" is rock solid.

Whether you decide to repair your home's deficiencies prior to listing in order to get top dollar when you sell, or choose to simply disclose deficiencies up front and price your home accordingly, it's a win-win situation for you as a seller. The buyer will be impressed with your honesty and you won't likely end up in court as a result of covering up a defect that immediately becomes problematic for the new owners after they take possession. There should be no surprises that arise as a result of the purchasers own inspection of your home. Remember I could be the home inspector hired to determine your home's condition for the purchasers. Most of my clients realize that they are vulnerable and often wearing their hearts on their sleeves when they fall in love with their "Dream Home". They hire me for another unbiased professional opinion. My job is very straight forward; to call it as I see it.

'The Seductive Power of Home Staging: A Seven-Step System for a Fast and Profitable Sale' is in my opinion, a <u>MUST READ</u> for anyone considering selling their home. Susan's insights and suggestions are all very solid and wise. This systematic guide will take you through everything you need to know to professionally stage your home – step by step. I plan on recommending it to all of my clients when doing their pre-listing inspections.

With Susan's assistance, show your home in the best light possible and you may be amazed with the results!

Paul Wilson - National Certificate Holder, PHPI, RHI
President – Home Inspectors and The Home Inspectors Institute
President – The Professional Home & Property Inspectors of Ontario
(PHPIO)

Acknowledgments

This book could not have happened without the support of my ever-enduring husband Gerry, who felt the anguish and joy of this project, and I thank him for his love and patience.

Special thanks to Paul Wilson, Registered Home Inspector (RHI) and member of the American Association of Home Inspectors (ASHI), and to Kimberley Seldon of Kimberley Seldon Design Group.

A sincere thank you is in order to my developmental editor, Donna Beech who provided an abundance of ideas and guidance, to Susan Kendrick who supplied direction and advice on my cover design, to John Eggen who kept me on track and to Evelyn Budd whose creative graphic design made my cover a reality.

Photographs were supplied in part by Darlene Hall-Barratt and Sophye Robert to whom I extend my thanks.

Scores of other people contributed to this book to whom I express my gratitude and appreciation. Support, information and ideas were contributed by my siblings, John and Peter Rowe and Sally Machell, my daughters Collette Taylor and Lorraine Escher, and my good friends and colleagues Bill Bezanson, Elsie Campbell, Mike Gillesie, Anthony Pearson, Angela Sutcliffe, Judith Cane, Lisa Larter, Nora Akkermans, Elizabeth Doherty, Lise Snedden, Andrea Fajrajsl, Annette Arents, Liz Doherty, Lawrence Northway, Linda Welsh, James Dundin, Bruce Brown, Barbara Langdon, Elizabeth Martwick, Denise Vierich, JP King, Susan Monaghan, Christie Cooke of Majority Marketing and Ken Haines, President of the Colour Wheel Company (www.colorwheelco.com),

I have not attempted to cite in the text all the authorities and sources consulted in the preparation of this book. To do so would require more space than is available. The list would include libraries, professional organizations, periodicals and many more individuals.

I sincerely thank all these wonderful people.

A Word from the Author

Staging your home is about getting the quickest, most lucrative sale possible. If you are thinking about selling your home – soon or even in the next 5 years – then *now* is the time to start thinking about how to prepare your home to appeal to the largest number of buyers out there.

If you think your home is ready to appeal to most buyers as it is right now, you are wrong.

How can I say this so confidently, when I haven't even been to your home? Well, because, first, I know that you have purchased furniture that you like or have inherited furniture that has sentimental value to you. I know that you made a decision to cover your windows with blinds or draperies that look really beautiful and probably cost a lot of your hard-earned money. Next, I know that you have warmed up your house with charming little curios and collections that you and your family love. You have painted or wallpapered your home in colours that make you feel comfortable.

Everyone does this. You don't decorate your home to appeal to your neighbours or the people you meet at the supermarket checkout. You do your best to create a warm, nurturing environment, tailor-made to suit your family.

When you are ready to sell, you have a different agenda. Your tastes and those of your family are not the first consideration. Instead, you want to set the stage so your home creates buyer interest. It is the best way to ensure that your home will sell for the highest possible price in today's market.

Selling your home in today's market is tougher than ever. If you are like most people, you don't move enough in your lifetime to acquire a lot of experience in preparing your home for re-sale. You know how to make it look warm and inviting for a dinner party or a sleep-over with your children's friends, but you don't have the training for turning your home into a showpiece that will generate optimum value. Don't worry. Knowing you need advice is the best place to start! You don't have to figure out everything yourself. Here at last is a book that will teach you about the practical side of making your home stand out from the competition.

As an avid researcher of interior decorating and theatrical set design, I have made it my business to study the connections between the two. I understand the problems that face homeowners; I have moved nineteen times in England

and Canada and know first-hand what it takes to stage a home, to make it *everyone's* home.

If you knew how to get more money from your house and sell it in a shorter amount of time by putting in some strategic effort and a few dollars – that you would be sure to get back, either by selling your home quickly and/or increasing the dollar value – wouldn't you be willing to give it a shot? Of course you would!

This book will take you through the steps to get to your goal – selling your house quickly for the maximum dollar value.

You may be thinking it would be nice to have a crystal ball to find out exactly who you are preparing your house for. If you knew that, you could deliberately add in elements they would like, repaint in colour schemes that you know will appeal to them and make the house a place they would want to call home. Does it surprise you to know that this is very possible? I don't have a crystal ball, but I can tell you who your customers are, what they are looking for, and how they will live in your home. They are not a lot different from you, but they, like you, want to start afresh in their new home. With home staging, you can create the home of their dreams, while selling your home for the price of *your* dreams. It's good for everyone.

Introduction

The Swinging Sixties

*"The secret to a rich life is to have
more beginnings than endings."*

~ David Weinbaum

It was England in the Swinging Sixties when I moved into a brand new house as a brand new bride. Our property was situated in a row of six newly built, small-terraced homes in an expanding "housing estate". Acacia Walk quickly filled with newlyweds like my husband and I. Everyone in our row became friends.

For many of us living in Acacia Walk, the mortgage took care of most of our hard-earned money and there was hardly anything left over for entertainment. And we were all anxious to get rid of the builder's boring beige. So one weekend, we made a block party out of painting our doors. To the competing sounds of the Beatles and the Rolling Stones, all six of us on our row wielded our borrowed paintbrushes and decorated our front doors. We splattered our flared jeans and psychedelic shirts, as we painted over our ugly, matching brown doors with fresh new colours that allowed us to revel in our fun-loving personalities and youth.

As a young couple we didn't have enough money to actually furnish our little pad, so we were very grateful when we were pitied by relatives who delivered furniture to our doorstep to help get us started. Of course none of the furniture matched and, frankly, it was fairly dreadful, but we were grateful nonetheless.

During the day I worked as a receptionist at a book-printing company and engaged in inspiring conversations with high-profile writers. Barbara Woodhouse, dog trainer extraordinaire and originator of the canine-call "Walkies!" was among the authors who frequently visited our company to watch as their books came hot off the press. Barbara was great company. We shared our ideas with energy and enthusiasm. I soon realized that I aspired to be like her one day.

Introduction

Sitting at the receptionist desk, I was expected to look neat and professional, while sounding educated and knowledgeable about the printing process and about what author wrote what book. Not everyone noticed, but I never used my hands when describing the printing process. I kept them hidden under the desk. Even Barbara never knew that this apparent model of demure, professional deportment was nothing of the sort. My hands were always covered with paint!

After work I flung all my receptionist responsibilities aside and morphed into an interior decorator. I was on a first-name basis at the local paint and fabric stores, lugging gallons of paint and rolls of coordinating fabrics onto the double-decker buses. I borrowed paint brushes from my dad and painted our donated furniture so it all matched. My mother-in-law lent me her old sewing machine. Having grown up with an antique treadle sewing machine, I was pleased to see that this one was more modern. It had a handle on the side to make the needle go up and down manually. With that awkward, but trusty, contraption, I sewed slip covers for our lumpy sofa. Since I really had no idea how do it, there were yards of fabric left over. I couldn't bear to let anything to go to waste, so – making obsession the mother of invention – I picked up wooden orange crates from the local outdoor market, brought them home on the bus and, with a little foam padding, stitched covers for them, transforming them into matching footstools.

When I was given 20 yards of beautiful silky fabric, which I sewed to make curtains for our living room, I thought I was in heaven. It turned out that my name was very apt. I was now the consummate Suzy Homemaker. Who knew? I painted the house from top to bottom in wonderful shades of gentle colours inspired by our fabric. When my work was complete, our house had finally become a home and we loved it.

Four years later, when our first child was on the way, we had the opportunity to buy a beautiful, new, single-family home in the country. I was so thrilled to be moving to a larger place and dreamed of how I would decorate this one. But living in this new home was conditional on us selling our little row house, so I set to work again.

With the intention of attracting buyers, I enthusiastically spruced up our terraced home ready for the viewing public. We had to sell this house quickly, if we were going to claim our dream home in the country. I polished the wooden parquet floor, touched up the delicate, gossamer-green paintwork and re-arranged the furniture so that buyers could move easily from room to room. The artwork was dusted. The bathroom was cleaned till it sparkled. The vacuum cleaner, feather dusters and tins of polish were relocated from the hall closet to the broom cupboard, which, up until then, had been crammed with old newspapers and half-full cans of paint. I bought macramé hangers from the thrift shop, filled them with trailing plants and affixed them to the ceiling. As a final touch I gathered flowers from my garden and displayed them in pretty vases throughout the home. It was my belief that putting out this effort would attract more buyers. This process did not have a name at the time, but we now know it to be home staging.

Putting our little terraced home up for sale would have been unbearable, if it had not been for the lure of our new country home. The details felt so overwhelming. The thought of giving people permission to wander through our rooms and having to listen to them making judgmental comments felt like a violation. In those days we didn't have the luxury of having a realtor to show visitors around, we had to do it ourselves. I worried that our house would not sell. My worrying was needless. The first couple who wandered through our home loved it so much that they wanted to buy it immediately. The furniture too! They actually wanted to pay money for my upholstered wooden crates! We had lots of people interested in our house over the course of the next few days and that first couple increased their offer substantially to secure the sale. We sold our house within two weeks – for more than the asking price! Staging our home had paid off.

What a joy it was to move into our house in the country so quickly! In our fresh new surroundings, our first task was to equip our kitchen. The kitchen was typical of new homes built in England in the late 60's. It had nothing in it. You would never see this today, but when we moved in, the kitchen had no cabinets, no countertops, no appliances and no flooring. It was just an empty room with plumbing sticking out of the wall. With a long list in hand, we shopped for everything, including –literally –the kitchen sink!

After our baby daughter was born, I became a stay-at-home mom and juggled the joy of caring for our baby with decorating our country home and planting a garden. We stayed in that house for two-and-a-half years before we had another opportunity that was so exciting that we simply could not turn it down. We had the chance to live and work in Canada.

Introduction

Moving abroad is a major undertaking. For us as a young couple, the task of coordinating the arrangements with my husband's new employers in Canada, working our way through the emigration protocol, packing up all our furniture for shipping across the Atlantic, and finding accommodations in Montreal, all while caring for a two-year-old and placating two sets of distressed grandparents, was much more demanding than we expected. To make things more complicated, we didn't have much time. The job offer was dependent on us moving right away.

As a result, we were unable to prepare our home for sale as I had done with our last home. We left our empty house in the hands of an estate agent and a solicitor. As we were leaving, I turned around to say goodbye to our house. For us, it had been a beautiful home, with gorgeous views, a flourishing garden and a marvelous kitchen, but now it looked sad and abandoned, empty and unloved. Without furniture – and all the things that make a house a home – it had lost its appeal.

Sadly, over the next eight months we were forced to drop the price of our beloved house in the country so many times that we were in danger of losing the value of everything we had put into it. Just before that happened, the estate agent found a buyer and almost gave it away to them for an outrageously low price. While I was relieved, the dramatic difference between the two house sales was starting to raise important questions in my mind. With two home sales behind me, I was far from being an expert, but I had a hunch that the effort I'd put into staging the first house had made all the difference.

Canada Quest

We intended to stay just two years. Montreal was our introduction. Suddenly, we found ourselves exposed to the French language, using a different currency, driving on the right side of the road, choosing from dozens of television stations and enjoying the extraordinary weather. It was an overwhelming and incredible experience.

In fact, we stayed three years in *la belle provence* before heading to Canada's beautiful Far North – with our energetic four year old and our beautiful six week old baby daughter. While I was in Whitehorse, Yukon, I discovered an interest in community theatre, designing costumes and creating realistic sets. It soon became a passion. After seven years of living above the 60th parallel, my husband was transferred, so we moved 5,660 kilometers to Canada's capital city, Ottawa.

I pursued my passion in theater in local Ottawa community theatre groups, gaining experience in creating costumes and sets for the stage. During the late eighties, when my husband and I went our separate ways, I rented a home just outside Ottawa with my two young daughters. We lived there happily for five years before my landlord told me that he would be selling the property. I was given first right of refusal to purchase the house, but the cost was far over my head. Out of pure habit, I staged the house – as I had done with every house I had lived in, except our country house – to help my landlord sell the home. His house sold in just two weeks. This was good news for my landlord, but bad news for me. My success had backfired! I had made the house so appealing that I'd created a challenge for myself: finding a new home without delay.

I was elated when I found a small three-story town home condominium in the growing city of Kanata, just twenty minutes from downtown Ottawa, Ontario. It had been on the market for a while. It was disheveled, scruffy and occupied by renters, but I was confident that I could spruce up this little place if the asking price were right. After some negotiation I proudly signed on the dotted line and became a landlady for three months.

It was only after I moved into this little house that I learned my first important lesson: never, ever skip the services of a building inspector. This house took on its own persona and I named it the House-From-Hell.

Numerous problems arose in the first few days which needed to be fixed immediately. These ranged from gaping holes in the walls (caused by my tenants having a fight) to broken water pipes and raw sewage backups; from a decayed wooden deck to waterlogged walls; from power blackouts to a furnace breakdown. The refrigerator was filled with some unidentifiable glob which had us all gagging while I cleaned it out. It took me six hours to scrub the ensuite bathroom.

Later that same day my beautiful, but shy, teenaged daughter decided to try out the shower. After twenty minutes, she realized that the drain was blocked and was not going to clear itself. Increasingly anxious, as the water rose above her knees, she had to make a humiliating decision. She could call for help, but that would mean I would rush upstairs and see her naked. Or she could preserve her modesty by opening the shower door, but that would allow a cascade of water to gush out the shower, into the bedroom and through the ceiling to the floors below. Her modesty prevailed. As the flood from the shower raced out of the bathroom, the globe light fixtures on floors below soon resembled goldfish bowls. So much water had accumulated that it ran down the walls and out into the street!

And the problems in my House-From-Hell continued to pile up. Over five years I more or less emptied my bank account on the house. We all suffered a lot of anguish, but gradually my little house was transformed, with reliable plumbing, updated deck, new carpeting and freshly tiled foyer. Every room had been painted in colours to match my furnishings and I had installed new, modern light fixtures. What more could be done?

During one swelteringly hot summer night, as I lay in my bed under a wet towel to keep cool, I acknowledged that the vision of installing air conditioning was next on the list. In spite of the appeal of deliciously cool air, it was one renovation too much. I determined then and there that this house was just not worth it. Enough was enough. On the spot, I decided to put my House-from Hell on the market.

Naturally, I prepared it for sale using my now time-tested techniques of home staging. Just as the "For Sale" sign was being hammered into my lawn I heard an echo. I turned to see my next-door-neighbours pounding in a "For Sale" sign on their own lawn. Wondering what I was up against, I visited my competition. Our house prices were the same. They had upgraded their home as had I, but our prospective homebuyers were going to be shopping in the hottest summer on record – and I don't mean house sales! This gave my neighbours a much bigger drawing card: air conditioning.

Now I was nervous. Very nervous. House sales were on the decline. It was stressful watching visitors compare our two houses. In my mind it was a certainty that my neighbour's house would be snapped up first. The air in their home was so deliciously cool!

When my house sold in three weeks, while theirs remained on the market, I was amazed, but my confidence in home staging grew to a new level. Even up against a miserable heat wave, home staging had won! As if I needed further validation, my buyers wanted all my window dressings – the ones I had purchased from the thrift shop – and my couch – because it went so well with the wall colour. Aha! My little home staging secrets had proven successful once again.

Introduction

In total, I have moved nineteen times – from England to Canada to Montreal to the Far North to Ottawa and everywhere in between. When preparing the houses for sale, I have always instinctively staged them, keeping a vision of the buyer's dreams and desires in mind. All the houses I have prepared for sale have sold quickly. When we were unable to prepare the country house in England, it took almost a *year* to sell.

It was not until many years later that I realized the connection between my ongoing passion for theatrical stage design and home staging. They both use the same principles. In theater, a good set design should be a backdrop to create an illusion that supports the playwright's vision. In selling a home, the furnishings should be a backdrop to showcase the architecture of the home and create a warm, comfortable environment. In both presenting a play and selling a home, you need to create an appeal that extends to a wide audience. It was a pleasure to realize I had been using these techniques instinctively all those years ago on Acacia Walk.

Since I have begun teaching others these home staging techniques, I have seen them work time and again with astonishing results. With this book, I will share with you the staging secrets that have proven successful on hundreds of homes.

PART ONE

Chapter One

The Definition of Home Staging

"All the world's a stage,
And all the men and women merely players:
They have their exits and their entrances;
And one man in his time plays many parts."

~ William Shakespeare

In this Chapter:

- What is home staging?
- Why is home staging so important?
- How to satisfy the most critical buyer.
- The Seven-Step System.
- The benefits of staging your home.
- The secrets of home staging.

Exciting things happen when you properly showcase your home. If you think a vase of flowers and a good cleaning are going to do it, think again. Getting your home ready for the public is different from just tidying up for a visit from the in-laws.

In this competitive real estate market, the bar has been raised to new levels. The popularity of the internet has revolutionized the approach in which people buy property. Buyers can view and compare hundreds of available homes online before they even step outside.

You need a different line of attack to make your home appeal to the largest possible audience. To compete in this market, you need more subtle – yet powerful – techniques to make your home stand out from the competition. As the saying goes, "You only get one chance to make a first impression." To sell quickly and for the most money, your home has to appeal to every viewer who steps through your door.

Furthermore, if you want to sell your home for the maximum money – and let's face it, who doesn't? – you need to get more than one person interested.

3

Nothing drives up a price faster than the perception that your home is in high demand.

Ultimately, the secret of selling your home quickly, for more money, lies in buyer perception. I will show you specific techniques for increasing the value perceived by the buyer. With a little care and attention, anyone can make their home more appealing. With home staging, you will make your home irresistible.

What is Home Staging? Home staging means preparing a house for resale; to appeal to the largest possible audience, for the highest possible price.

As soon as you know or have made the decision to move house you must start looking at your house through the buyer's eyes. You might not be moving for five years or it could be as soon as next month, either way it is important to start preparing your home to its best possible potential; particularly before the pictures are taken, before the home is put on the market and before your first viewers visit the house. You want potential buyers to see your castle at its very best from the get go.

Home staging is often confused with interior decorating, but in fact they are polar opposites. Staging involves a creating an effect – a tasteful combination of colours, textures and placement of furniture and accessories– both inside and outside the home. It means ensuring all problems in the home are fixed and that the house is cleaned and polished from top to bottom with no surface left untouched. It involves removing wallpaper, decals and stenciled borders – painting walls and other surfaces, selecting and arranging furniture layout and replacing outdated fixtures.

Interior decorating, meanwhile, focuses attention on decorating and renovating, specifically to the homeowners personal style and individuality.

When you're selling your home, you need to remove enough of *your* personality from the home to give the buyer enough space that they can imagine *themselves* living there. You do not want potential buyers to be distracted by the highly personal or controversial items you might have added to suit your interior decorating style.

As a seller the first thing you must do is to start thinking of your home as a house. A commodity. A product. This is the most difficult thing you will have to do, but doing this will allow you to pull away from the emotional ties that frequently hold you hostage. This is a very important part of the selling process as it will make it easier to understand and see your home through a buyer's eyes – but not any old buyer. Your goal is to impress the most critical buyer. The critical buyer will look for any occasion to lower the price, so we must remove that possibility.

The secret is knowing how much to take out and how much to leave in. Going overboard and making the home so empty and sterile that medical surgery could be performed on the kitchen table, is a put off for many buyers. It's important to find the right balance.

The key is: *neutralizing, but not sterilizing* your home's décor so your potential buyers can visualize themselves living happily there.

Why is Home Staging So Important? We don't always know why we like or dislike something. Often, we just know that it feels right or it doesn't. If we can't articulate why something does or doesn't feel right we call it a gut feeling. If it doesn't feel right, we move on.

Exactly the same thing happens when prospective buyers view your home. It's an important purchase, requiring one of the biggest financial investments most people will ever make. And yet, ultimately, the deciding factor that makes people pick one house over another is a gut feeling.

With its theatrical roots in creating crowd-pleasing performances, home staging goes further than design or decorating or neat-and-tidy. It reaches for those elusive qualities of charm and attraction that make people want it, without even knowing why.

Studies show that staged homes sell faster – within 32 to 42 days – and sell for 3% to 20% more money. A $300,000 home where the owners have taken the time to do home staging to make it feel fresh and alluring can increase its appeal in a way that shows up in the sales price – bringing $9,000 to $60,000 more than a comparable house without staging.

How to Satisfy the Most Critical Buyer. Your primary goal is to stir an emotion in even the most critical buyers. Ask yourself: When critical buyers view your home, what will they see? What will they say?

The thought of having strangers wandering through your home, peering into cupboards and closets and making comments can be unsettling. Nothing could be more natural than for you to believe that everyone will like your home as is. It's decorated to your style, filled with your cherished possessions, your personality and, most importantly, your memories. Your friends and relatives will tell you your home is beautiful and nothing needs to be done to make it better. They mean well and, frankly, it feels nice to receive all those compliments, but let's face it, when they visit, it is you they come to see. They have never come to analyze, evaluate and critique your home. They are usually not potential buyers. And, to be perfectly honest, unless they are a home staging professional, they are not trained to see the home through the eyes of a critical buyer.

In the old days, before the internet, your home would be listed in a catalog as thick as a New York telephone book. There was no way for buyers to effectively compare properties without actually going from house-to-house. Buying a house was quite a chore. Some buyers preferred to end the process as quickly as possible. If they saw any house they liked in a suitable neighbourhood, they snapped it up without delay. The task of finding out what else was out there was so overwhelming that most people just took what they could get.

Those days are gone. With the internet at people's fingertips, buyers can stay up all night researching neighbourhoods and looking at photographs. It is recommended the changes you decide upon in your home should be completed *before* photographs are taken and posted on list sheets or web sites. Allow the pictures to be true. Your photographs will be loaded with subliminal messages. The way the room is furnished, the layout, the lighting, etc. Unfortunately, not all those messages come across in a positive light. Buyers who are looking for wide open spaces are put off when they see that the rooms are actually quite small and cramped. To deceive with super-wide angle photographs give the false impression the home is larger than it really is and wastes everybody's time. Raising the bar on reality will not impress buyers; to the contrary it will drive them away.

A friend of mine once received a debilitating subliminal message that made her a flying-phobic. The very first time she ever sat down in her seat on an airplane, she saw a coffee stain in the middle of the pull-down tray. Being a careful, meticulous housekeeper herself, she deduced that if the staff were too busy to clean up a simple coffee ring, then what guarantee did she have that the plane's engine was maintained? She exited the plane before it took off and couldn't be persuaded to get on another one for years! A neglected coffee stain was a showstopper for her.

The same can hold true for house buyers. The subliminal thought that goes through a person's mind is this: If the owners haven't the time to maintain the parts you *can* see, they surely haven't taken care of the parts you *can't* see. They may exit your house without another word and you will have missed the opportunity to sell them your home.

As an analogy, people will happily buy brand new furniture or – at the other end of the spectrum – antique furniture. But nobody wants to buy old, shabby, worn-out furniture – unless it is at a garage sale for a rock bottom price. Translate this reality to your biggest investment: your house. Buyers will either spend money on a newly built home with brand new features or a beautiful old home full of character and charm, but they will not spend their money on an old, shabby and worn out house – unless they are getting it at a rock-bottom price.

If a viewer is not interested in the home they have just visited, the realtors will ask what it was specifically that they did not like about the property. Most often, the viewers will respond that they don't exactly know, they cannot put their finger on it. This means it's time to attend to the fine detail in your home.

How to Stage Your Home: A Seven-Step System. In this book, you will learn a powerful, seven-step-system to help you view the home as a highly critical buyer would see it. Each of these steps will help you refine your vision until you create a home that is truly irresistible to the most buyers possible.

The Seven-Step System has been designed to evaluate each individual area and room in your home. Using each of the seven elements in every room will bring your home to its maximum potential. The combination of all seven steps creates a powerful force. It will create the image of a whole lifestyle of wellbeing with a welcoming feel from people living there, enhancing your home's charm and personality. Sellers need to understand that the way we live in our home is not the way we sell our home

So you are wondering how I can recommend you dress up your home without ever having seen it. Breaking the tasks of staging your home into manageable chunks allows you to focus on one detail at a time. It does not matter how big, small, complex or simple your rooms might be. The principles of this methodical approach are the same for every home.

Use this system to focus on your target market and attract interested buyers within days of putting your home on the market.

The biggest secret is that it should never be obvious that the home is staged. An obvious staging will leave the buyer feeling deceived. Nobody likes to be hoodwinked and doing this could result in a missed sale. Following each of the seven elements precisely allows your home to maintain a modicum of personality while allowing enough scope for the buyer to develop an emotional connection, which is the key to a successful sale.

Just as in the theater, illusions are designed to create a seductive mood that will appeal to a wide audience. Staging a home is about using as many effects as possible to make the home look more interesting and attractive all while drawing the eye to the architectural jewels of the home.

You will also learn specific techniques that will help you create the right environment quickly – at the lowest cost. You will find out what is important to the buyer, what is the optimal way to arrange existing furniture and accessories, what colours to choose, what to take out and what to leave in to make your home more appealing.

The Benefits of Staging Your Home. Two unexpected additional benefits have been reported after staging a home. One is that homeowners have found that short notice preparation for their showing was faster, and they were confident when the call came that they knew the drill and could quickly leave the property secure in the knowledge that the home showed to its best potential. The other benefit has shown that because of prior preparation, sellers are less stressed, and better mentally and physically organized for the move to their new location.

The Secrets of Home Staging. Staging is theatre. It is all about creating illusions. It is not about covering up serious problems that the new homeowner will need to know about, but about showing the home you love in its best possible light.

After so many years creating persuasive illusions on stage, I have learned ways to use clever lighting, remarkable colours, airy spaces and bold accessories to make rooms appear larger or taller, more spacious or cozier. I have written this book to share with you some of my most treasured theatrical secrets.

Chapter Two

When to Renovate

"A house is made of walls and beams;
a home is made of love and dreams."

~ Anonymous

In this Chapter:

- Kitchen and bathroom renovations.
- Landscaping and painting.
- Technology updates.
- Renovations that offer little or no payback.

When you look at your home with a critical eye, where do you think you can best spend your decorating or renovating dollars? There's no point in spending a fortune on renovating for a dream kitchen or bathroom for the people who live there after you've gone, unless the efforts are going to reap financial benefits for you. Inspect before you renovate: Find out if there are any major defects requiring replacement, repairs or upgrades before you start your renovations.

In Canada, the Appraisal Institute specialists have compared the most common renovations and evaluated which ones are most likely to be worthwhile, when you're selling your home. The top ten renovations that will bring you the best potential for return are:

1. Paint and décor – 73%

2. Kitchen renovation – 72%

3. Bathroom renovation – 68%

4. Exterior painting – 65%

5. Upgrading flooring – 62%

6. Replacing windows or doors – 57%

7. Main floor family room addition – 51%

8. Fireplace addition – 50%

9. Basement renovation – 49%

10. Furnace/heating system replacement – 48%

Three of the top four most requested renovations, coincidentally, provide the best payback; kitchen, bathroom, and exterior painting. The fourth most requested renovation is landscaping, which has a payback of 30%-60%

In each of these areas, some changes give you more value than others. Let's look more closely at the top four.

Kitchen and Bathroom Renovations. The kitchen is regarded the heart of the home, the place where guests gather and fine meals are created. Take special care to make your kitchen spectacular. Allow your buyers to imagine themselves entertaining their own friends and relatives there.

You don't have to spend a fortune to make your kitchen stand out. Even small changes can add new life. Replacing old handles, knobs, faucets and light fixtures makes a world of difference. Replacing a worn laminate countertop is also a great idea for a low-cost, high-impact update. Cleanliness and good lighting are essential, as is a good sized food preparation area, good quality flooring and updated fixtures. In the case of kitchens, payback can be as high as 200%.

If your kitchen is more than 40 years old, you may want to consider the potential value of completely remodeling the area. Kitchen renovations generally start at about $10,000. It all depends on the quality of what you install. Working in the heart of the home and updating the kitchen is always an ambitious project but might be more beneficial than just superficial updates. First prepare a budget, plan the layout and finishes and hire an expert installer. A profitable kitchen renovation hinges on four factors: adequate budget, proper planning, quality materials and an expert installer. First, write down the list of all the areas that need to be updated. It is said that "the devil is in the details," so make sure you consider every single facet. And don't forget to find out if you need a construction permit from your municipality.

Inspect your bathroom carefully. Potential buyers must be able to imagine taking a shower in your bathroom. Mould in the grout is easy to fix and repainting the bathroom does wonders. The cost to upgrade the cabinet knobs and handles, lighting fixtures, faucets and installing a brand-new toilet seat is low and the payback enormous.

For a bathroom upgrade, it generally cost no less than $5,000 to do properly and if you have an expensive taste, it can cost considerably more. It is very important to work out a budget and stay on track as with most upgrades dollars have a habit of running amok.

Landscaping and Painting. Landscaping and exterior painting add great curb appeal. Remember that the external area of your home will give your buyer the first impressions. Make those first impressions count.

Simple, superficial landscaping improvements – such as trimming trees or mowing the lawn – can give the grounds a freshness they didn't have before. Plant flowers and sweep the pathways to show the buyer that the people who live in this house really care about their property. This will further reinforce their sense that the home has been maintained.

A fresh coat of paint has the least outlay – reaping a 73% return on the dollar – for maximum appeal. It might be more cost effective to hire a good quality professional painter. In the long run, it may be cheaper than doing it yourself. Professional painters prepare surfaces, use quality paint, work quickly and clean up before they go.

Repainting the fence, the garage doors and the front door all give exceptionally good return for very minimal time and investment. Window and door trim including shutters should all be scrutinized.

Impress your buyers right off the bat with a beautiful entrance by putting a fresh coat of paint on the front door. The front door is the entrance to your home. It should not only be welcoming, but distinctive. If you can find a tasteful way to make it stand out – such as adding trim, a door knocker, and a new doorknob – it will be well worth your effort.

The garage doors should never be painted the same colour as the front door. Why make the garage doors stand out? That might be the usual entrance when you are parking the car and carrying in all the groceries, but for your guests the appropriate entrance is the front door. The garage doors should be painted to blend in with the house colour, whether it is brick, siding or cedar.

On the interior of your home, repainting the walls, baseboards and trim will make the rooms seem refreshed. In high traffic areas – such as a hallway, family room, children's room, bathroom and kitchen – use a pearl or a satin finish to make cleaning easier. Matt or flat paint on walls in the living room or master bedroom will create a rich, luxurious look. Semi-gloss paint on the woodwork will make cleaning simple; it also makes the room appear more spacious. Stay away from high gloss paint unless the surface is in super good shape, as it will show imperfections.

Technology Updates. Technology is hot. Incorporating some of the latest technology can make your home seem more exciting than the rest. It can create a feeling of high quality, and state-of-the-art innovation can greatly increase the perceived value of your home.

Before you go tech-crazy, keep a couple of things in mind:

- A few hundred dollars spent on tech products will probably not make a multimillion-dollar home stand out.
- Overspending on a starter or mid-priced home might differenti-ate it from the competition, but you will probably not recuper-ate the cost.

The top two tech trends are sure to make potential buyers remember your home:

- A widescreen, high-definition TV that can be mounted under a kitchen cabinet and can be folded away out of sight.
- A deadbolt door lock with biosensors to read your fingerprints for the latest in security.

Gadgets, such as remote control light dimmers and electrical outlets or a wireless home control and automation system that turn on the lights and heater before you enter the house are cool, yet practical. These systems are available for every use and every budget. Be sure to explain the value of the special features to your potential buyers. For a few hundred dollars and a couple hours of your time, you can entice buyers to enjoy the ultimate con-venience and safety provided by these systems.

- Flat panel televisions mounted in or on the walls. Both LCD and plasma monitors have been around for a few years, but since so many people haven't bought them yet, they still draw attention.
- A wire concealment system to hide your cables and cords with a "spine" or "ribbon" that blends with the colour of the wall.

- A multi-room, digital sound system that lets you listen to the same or different music in various parts of the house.
- Window coverings with motorized shades, blinds or drapes can really add the "Wow!" factor. Press a button to automatically open or close them. Some products will even open or close at a specific time each day. The cost is about $1,000 per window.

If you do install some of these items, it is important to leave short, concise directions, telling the new owners how to use these high tech toys.

Renovations that Offer Little or No Payback. The following renovations offer little or no payback and can even decrease the value of the home. Many an enthusiastic renovator has spent a lot of money, only to be disappointed in the return on these items.

- In-ground swimming pools are never a great selling feature. Generally they add very little to the value. If the pool is in bad condition, they most certainly will detract.
- A do-it-yourself renovation of poor quality or design will decrease value.
- Expensive, high-end upgrades in a small house in a low-end neighbourhood will never be able to pay for themselves.
- A major basement renovation in a large house will give very little return, compared to the cost.

Knowing which renovations will raise the appeal of your home and which result in needless expense can save you literally tens of thousands of dollars. Always remember, you are renovating the home to appeal to your buyers, not yourself. You may have always wanted to live in a house with a swimming pool, but if the statistics show that most people find a pool a liability, your money will be better spent elsewhere.

Chapter Three

Your Target Market

*"There is nothing half so pleasant
as coming home again."*

~ Margaret Elizabeth Sangster

In this Chapter:

- Getting to know your buyers.
- Ready-to-move-in buyers.
- Fixer-upper buyers.
- The female touch.

Preparing your home for your buyers has become an art. And as history shows us, some artists toil in obscurity their whole lives and never sell a painting, while others make a thriving career painting pieces that are appreciated and treasured by the public. Clearly, when it comes to home staging, you want your efforts to have strong appeal to the buying public. In order to do that, you must know your market.

Getting to Know Your Buyers. So who are these buyers? What do they like? What are their buying habits? To sell anything, particularly a home, it is important to know your target market. You need to know exactly what it takes to make these people say "Wow!!"

In my experience, there are the two categories of buyers shopping for homes: ready-to-move-in buyers and fixer-upper buyers.

Ready-to-Move-in Buyers. Buyers who want a fresh, clean home for themselves are ready-to-move-in buyers. They do not want to start decorating or renovating. They want to move in or rent the property out immediately. This ready-to-move-in mindset amounts to approximately 90% of people in the home buying market.

These buyers will only consider purchasing a home in move-in condition. If they see any flaws, they'll either walk away or start complaining. Because they don't want to have to fix anything, they tend to overestimate how much work it will be. As a result, they will argue that the price should be reduced by 15-25%, because of the time, money and aggravation they are about to incur.

Fixer-Upper Buyers. The remaining 10% are homebuyers hungry to make a deal on what they perceive to be a "handyman special" or a "fixer-upper" and they want the price to reflect that. Some may only be able to afford a fixer upper. They assume that the best way for them to get into a house is to buy something that needs work. They are willing to spend their time and thousands of dollars at every phase to create their dream home.

Among the fixer-upper buyers are a group of people planning to buy a house at rock bottom prices and then hastily renovating it for resale. This is called "flipping". Buy low. Fix up. Sell high. In effect, these people are making a healthy profit by combining real estate investment with home staging.

90% of buyers want ready-to-move-in, 10% are looking for handyman specials.

The Female Touch. Studies show that women influence 80% to 90% of all consumer purchases. Many reading this would argue that women influence closer to 99% of home purchases. Men buying a home are strongly influenced by the opinions of women, whether they're moving into that home with them or not.

Just before my single brother signed on the dotted line for a house he was interested in, he decided at the last minute to ask the opinion of a friend. When she saw the house, she pointed out a number of flaws. Once he heard her opinion, he decided not to buy the house and walked away.

If women influence 80% to 90% of all home purchases, wouldn't it be good to know their buying habits? Generally speaking, when it comes to a home, women are detail oriented. They notice more. Woman often ask about details that men may not perceive as important.

Have you noticed that men and women tend to shop differently? Men seem to place more importance on achieving their shopping objectives as "efficiently" as possible, whereas women tend to make their decisions in a broader sweep. Research shows that, instead of being satisfied with the question, "Does this solve the problem?" women tend to consider additional criteria: "Is this product going to be easy to use?" "How do I know this is the perfect decision?" "Have I fully considered all the options?"

It is not uncommon for men to buy a widescreen TV because it suits their needs, without thinking about how or whether it suits their home. Women, on the other hand, are more likely to ask how does this fit into my life.

So it appears that your target buyer is most likely a ready-to-move-in buyer who is either a woman or someone strongly influenced by a woman. Knowing this, doesn't it make sense that – in order to sell your home quickly, for the most money possible – you should focus on that target market?

Chapter Four

Tools of the Trade

*"Home is an invention
upon which no one has ever improved."*

~ Ann Douglas

In this Chapter:

- Finding storage solutions.
- Why a colour fan deck is so useful.
- How to use a colour wheel.
- When to use a compass.
- Buying the right tape measure.
- The advantages of digital cameras.

You may never have pictured yourself as the type to strut around the grounds of a property in leather work boots and a tool belt, but you'll soon find that home staging is very hands on. The work boots are up to you, but I have to admit that some sort of carrying case will come in handy, because you're going to need to have the following tools on hand. You will be using them throughout the entire staging process.

Finding Storage Solutions. Purchase a box of black garbage bags, a box of yellow garbage bags, a collection of same-size cardboard boxes and several plastic dollar store baskets. You will learn where to use these supplies in *Step Two –Clutter* section.

Why a Colour Fan Deck is so Useful. Finding new colour for your home can be exciting, but it can also be daunting. Have you ever gone to the paint store, eager to choose a new colour, and then felt overwhelmed by the sheer magnitude of the choices available?

A colour fan deck allows you to take hundreds of those colours with you, so you can decide which wall colour will coordinate best with your floral-patterned sofa or perfectly accent your master bedroom or make sure the trim in the dining room complements the walls. The colour fan deck's compact size allows you to take it along with you on your home decorating shopping trips. You can find your own colour fan deck at any big box store, paint store, or online. You will learn more about how and where to use this tool in the *Step Four - Colour* section.

The Usefulness of a Colour Wheel. This practical tool takes the guesswork out of choosing colours. Although the Colour Wheel has just 12 colours, the colours vary continuously around the wheel with millions of possible shades.

Not only does the wheel show clearly which shades and tones complement each other, it also associates each colour with a perception. Colours have such a strong impact on the way people feel and act that is important to consider what effect your colour choices will have in the area being decorated.

You will learn more the colour wheel and colour terms in the *Step Four - Colour* section.

When to Use a Compass. A compass will allow you to confirm the directional aspect of the home. When it comes to making colour choices and selecting lighting, it is important to know what rooms face north, east, south or west. Using the Northern Hemisphere as an example, south facing rooms receive the "purest" light for most of the day, so the colours are seen as fairly true. North facing rooms tend to have "cold" light all day. Eastern and western rooms have changing light.

The Sun can be used for an approximate orientation, if you know the general time of day. In the morning, the Sun is in the east. Around noon, it is in the south in the Northern Hemisphere or in the north in the Southern Hemisphere. After noon, the Sun sets in the west. Most homeowners know where the sun rises and sets in their own home, but if the homeowners are not available to ask, you will be able to tell with a compass– even if it is dark or cloudy outside. Just remember, **Never Eat Slimy Worms** (North, East, South, West) and you'll be able to make the most of your compass. We will be using the compass in *Step Four –Colour*.

> **TIPS: Compass Trivia:** You can do away with the compass if you have an analogue watch face. The Sun in the sky revolves over 24 hours; the hour hand of your watch counts twelve hours. Assuming you are in the Northern Hemisphere, rotate the watch so that the hour hand points towards the Sun. The point halfway between the hour hand and 12 o'clock is south. There will be minor inaccuracies

due to the difference between local time and zone time, and due to the equation of time. During daylight saving time, for instance, the same method can be used using 11 instead of 12 o'clock.

Buying the Right Tape Measure. Purchase a good quality 20ft-25ft (6m-7m) metal, retractable tape measure that extends to at least 9ft (2.5m) before it "breaks". (When a metal tape measure is extended to a certain length without support, it will gently bend until it cannot support its own weight. At this point you will hear a loud crack; this is called a "break".)

The tape measure should have a locking mechanism that will allow you to pull out the length of tape you need, then lock, so it won't retract until it's unlocked.

This tape measure will allow you to take measurements by yourself, when help is not around. It can be used for measuring dimensions of rooms, ceiling height, furniture, windows, passage ways, lighting height, etc. You will be using this tool in *Step Six –Space Planning.*

The Advantages of Digital Cameras. Strangely enough, you can sometimes see much more clearly how to improve a room's layout, accessories and artwork placement by looking at its photograph, than you can if you are standing in the very room in which you took the picture!

A digital camera is invaluable for taking shots of the room to judge how you might improve it. It is also handy for the before and after pictures.

Take a shot from every corner of the room. Be sure that you have captured all the angles. You will be using the digital camera at the beginning, middle and end of the *Seven- Step System.*

PART TWO

Chapter Five

The Seven Steps

*"The indispensable first step in
getting the things you want out of life is this:
Decide what you want."*

~ Ben Stein

The Seven-Step System comprises:

1. RED FLAGS
    *   Identifying the problems that suggest your home has not been maintained which will stall or prevent a sale.
2. CLUTTER
    *   This is the visual noise that creates confusion. How to identify and deal with clutter.
3. FOCAL POINTS
    *   Bringing the eye to the benefits and features of your home.
4. COLOUR
    *   The secret of the colour that appeals to the majority of people is uncovered in this chapter.
5. LIGHTING
    *   Theatrical secrets are revealed to highlight those areas on which areas you want your homebuyers to focus.
6. SPACE PLANNING
    *   Making sense of the layout and purpose of each room and how to create illusions of openness and breathing space.
7. FINISHING TOUCHES
    *   Making your home stand out and more appealing to your buyers, including the addition of memory hooks.

STEP ONE – RED FLAGS

"Last night I lay in bed looking up
at the stars in the sky and I thought to myself,
where the heck is the ceiling?"

~ Anonymous

When I am designing a set for the theatre, I am very mindful to make the set authentic to the script and to the playwright's vision, but more importantly that everything works the way it intended to work. If the audience is distracted by disjointed seams on the flats (that's theatre-speak for walls), or the stairs creak, or a raised floor sounds hollow when walked upon, or the doors don't hold closed when they supposed to, then the enjoyment of the play can be spoiled. Building a realistic, convincing, safe and secure set is paramount to the relaxation and enjoyment of the audience. They can sit back and relax, allowing themselves to be transported into another world.

It's the same in your home. Problems, otherwise known as Red Flags, relate to the sound structure of the house. It's only after your buyers determine that it has been well maintained and is safe and secure that they will relax and allow themselves to build an emotional connection.

Looking for Red Flags is, without doubt, the single most critically important step in staging your home. Unattended Red Flags suggest to a buyer that your home has not been maintained. These things may not have troubled you while you were living in your home, but to a potential buyer, unresolved problems are showstoppers that can stall or prevent a sale entirely.

It is only after the Red Flags have been identified and addressed that we are able to continue with the remaining six steps. Red Flags have two levels.

Level One: Obvious Problems. Problems found in and around your home that you meant to fix but didn't find the time. The obvious problems are well known to you and usually easy to fix but might need special tools to put right. If you don't have the tools or you need specialized knowledge or don't have dedicated time you should call in the professionals. When it comes to selling your home, an unresolved problem could be the barrier or hurdle that is impossible for the buyer to overcome. This could mean a missed sale.

Level Two: Hidden Problems. Hidden problems are best revealed by a professional, registered home inspector. Your buyer is likely to call one too, but you can hire a home inspector yourself to come by for a pre-inspection. If you want to find out the hidden problems, it's an excellent idea.

Choose your home inspector wisely. There is currently no mandatory certification and no legislated requirement for home inspectors to take any courses or pass any tests. Anyone can hang out a shingle saying they are a home inspector, despite the fact that this is an occupation that requires special training, knowledge and good communication skills.

Mike Holmes' book *Holmes Inspection* describes some inspectors as fly-by-night unqualified charlatans posing as home inspectors and duping the public. He encountered many of them personally in the renovation business.

Check out industry associations which have set standards of practice and code of ethics that their members must adhere to. Before you hire an inspector, ask around for referrals and check their credentials. Hiring an unqualified inspector is worse than not hiring one at all.

While CMHC (Canada Mortgage & Housing Corporation) cannot endorse any one home inspector or association in Canada, they strongly recommend that consumers look to a professional association such as CAHPI – The Canadian Association of Home and Property Inspectors (www.cahpi.ca). CAHPI has strict educational requirements, standards of practice and code of ethics that their membership must adhere to through their membership with the CAHPI Provincial Chapters that span all across Canada. While provincial requirements may vary slightly, all qualified CAHPI members are designated as Registered Home Inspectors with the (RHI) designation. There is however, a new designation, truly national in scope and available through CAHPI, which has "raised the bar" for the home inspection profession in Canada - the National Certificate Holder, CAHPI with the support of CMHC, Human Resources and Social Development Canada and the Construction Sector Council, developed a national accreditation and certification program to help ensure the competency and professionalism of home inspectors all across Canada. Home Inspectors, who have met the requirements of this national program, are designated as National Certificate Holders (NCH). National Certificate holders must not only complete technical training requirements, they are also required to demonstrate their inspection skills in front of a Technical Inspection Peer Review (TIPR Board) and must be re-tested on a regular basis to ensure that their skills and knowledge remain current. This is why the National Certification Program's designation is now considered the "Gold Standard" for home inspectors across Canada.

In Ontario, Canada, many National Certificate Holders belong to The Professional Home and Property Inspectors of Ontario – PHPIO (www.phpio.ca), an association dedicated to the promotion of the national certification program by making it available to all inspectors across the province. In addition to holding the National Certificate Holder designation, qualified PHPIO's members also hold the Professional Home & Property Inspector – PHPI designation and are field tested regularly in order to maintain their designation. You can be confident in hiring a qualified professional home inspector if they have the National Certificate Holder designation from CAHPI.

It may sound like a good idea, but do not be tempted to hire an inspector recommended by your real estate representative. This is a conflict of interest. Your real estate representative may give you three recommendations, but you are not obligated to hire any one of them and can retain the services of the one you prefer. Buying a home is generally one of the largest investments a person will make in their life time. Anyone buying your home will likely want to hire the most experienced, and toughest professional home inspector their money can buy – for this reason alone – so should you!

The inspector will start his analysis from the curb to the front, sides and rear yards, up to the roof, through the house from the basement to the attic. After the walk-about, you should be given a written report of the found defects; do not be satisfied with a verbal report. Steer clear of a home inspector who offers to carry out repairs himself or gives you a business card recommendation. This is also conflict of interest.

A professional home inspector is qualified to uncover defects in and around your property which, when identified to a buyer, could be the setback to stall your sale. You can make the decision to either fix the situation or to disclose it to your buyer. Disclosure will put you in a negotiation position with your buyer.

So why would you shell out your money for a home inspector when the buyer will most certainly be hiring one? When you identify and carry out repairs before the home is listed, the buyer will see a well-maintained home and be excited about making an offer. If you decide to leave the issues of discovery up to the buyer the onus will still be on your shoulders to take care of the obstacles. If you consult with the buyer there is a high likelihood the buyer will estimate the rate of repair as far costlier than it really is and start hard negotiations to complete the sale at the lowest price possible or walk away from the sale.

Taking Down the Red Flags. Start with the obvious problems. One room or area at a time, list the jobs you have been meaning to do or started but never finished. With a pen and clipboard in hand and wearing your hypothetical Black-Hat-of-Doom, write down every obvious evil that needs attention.

Then take a bold course of action. Delegate the large jobs to competent family members, friends or to a skilled professional. If you are not qualified to tackle the job, do not even attempt to do it; leave it to the experts. If you botch the job, you will be short changing yourself (literally), when you come to sell your home. Check off every repair as you complete it.

Dirt and Grime. A major Red Flag that is often overlooked is dirt and grime. Most buyers are put off by dirt. Aren't you? For maximum curb appeal, sweep the pathways and use a pressure washer to get rid of any stains on the siding, driveways and walkways. Polish the windows, dust cobwebs from the porch, shake out the welcome mat, or buy a new welcome mat (the word *welcome* is a subliminal message).

If you have a pool, make sure that it is crystal clear and looks inviting. In the winter months, ensure that it has been closed properly for the season.

Inside the house, scrutinize each room. Take special notice of the bathroom and kitchen for mold and grime. Look around faucets, baseboards, inside cupboards under the sink; check around light fixtures for dust and bugs, vacuum behind furniture and kitchen appliances. I can hear you saying, "Buyers won't be looking behind my fridge and stove." No they probably won't, but accumulated dirt, dust and grime will be greasy and smelly, so pull out the appliances and wash walls and floors. Your home has to be sparkling clean, free of grease, grime, fingerprints, spills, stains, smudges, cobwebs and bugs.

Look in and around your furnace. Dirt is its biggest enemy, affecting the three basic components of your furnace, the filter system, the blower, and the motor. You can replace the furnace filters yourself, and thereafter about once a month during periods of continuous use but have the professionals take care of the blower and motor to maintain efficient use of fuel.

All this work might sound overwhelming. If so, it may be more satisfying – and cost effective – to hire professional cleaners to tackle the job. This is not a time for you to get stressed out.

Dirt creeps up on you. It's a fact. Beat it back and make your home as squeaky clean as it can be. Make it cleaner than your buyer's own home and your buyer will be even more anxious to move in right away!

> **TIPS: Dryer Sheet Value.** Dryer sheets can be used to wipe soap scum from a shower door. They also eliminate static cling in places other than the dryer. Use them to wipe television screens and monitors, attract loose pet hairs, clean Venetian blinds and wipe up sawdust after sand papering, and in the workshop.

Smells. Unfamiliar smells are another big Red Flag. They could be due to dust and dirt, cigarette smoke, pets, mold, etc. Smells are signs that the home is suffering with neglect. Get to the root cause of the smell. Invite a trusted friend into your home and ask them for an honest analysis of what they can smell. Some ethnic cooking, onions and cruciferous veggies are odiferous. Avoid highly pungent foods while your home is on the market. You want your home to smell fresh and clean.

When you deep clean and polish, you get rid of smells. Stuffy, dusty smells are a real turn-off. Make sure every corner of your home – including the uppermost corners of your ceilings – are free of dust and dirt. Lace curtains and soft furnishings often harbour dusty, musty smells.

Homebuyers are on the look out for any flaw in your home. Heavily scented products such as aerosol air fresheners, or plug-ins, often set these homebuyer's on high alert for flaws. They begin asking questions such as, what smell are they trying to cover up?

Allowing buyers to follow this line of thinking means they will be more critical of your home as they view it. Those with respiratory issues may actually have to leave without ever having the opportunity to view your home. Essentially, you have inadvertently hindered the sale process.

While we are on the subject of smells, let me share with you another story about my House-From-Hell. I am a non-smoker. When I was preparing my house in Kanata for sale, I noticed there was an offensive cigarette smell coming in from my neighbour's adjoining property into my furnace room. My neighbour smoked in his furnace room and his smoke was sucked through a little hole, picked up by my furnace and distributed throughout my house.

When I politely pointed this out to my neighbour, he ignored me. I took it up a notch. The condominium property manager sent around a man who claimed he could not smell a thing. Of course he couldn't; the man was a smoker and was used to the smell. Cranking it up further, I demanded a non-smoking contractor. This man could easily smell the smoke. He located the opening in the furnace room wall and blocked it. With that problem solved, I could comfortably put my house on the market. If you do have a problem with odors of some kind, solve it before it has a chance to become a viewer's Red Flag!

Your viewers should not have to wear one of these!

> **TIPS: For Bad Smells:** One secret to getting rid of smells is to light a good quality candle such as beeswax prior to a showing. Beeswax candles are very effective in eliminating unpleasant smells. Extinguish candles before your viewers arrive.

Creepy Crawlies. Bugs and rodents are Red Flags that will have your viewers running out the door. Never let your potential buyer see evidence of a bug problem, whether it is the critter itself or opened packages of ant killer, mouse traps, dead flies, bugs or spiders.

Once I was called in to help a homeowner prepare their home for sale. It had been on the market for almost a year. There was obviously a creature infestation. Ant traps, earwig bait, and mousetraps could be found in every corner of the house. The laundry room cabinets were full of aerosol fly and mosquito sprays and sticky paper to catch the moths.

A good solution to an ant problem is to pile cornmeal near their home. They love it and will carry it back to their nests, but they can't digest it. Sprinkling cinnamon around the house also works. Ants hate the smell.

> **TIPS: For Creepy Crawlies.** Get out those dryer sheets again. Their strangely fragrant, but unnatural, scent is a natural repellent to wasps, bees and mosquitoes outside your house and can keep ants, moths and even mice from coming in.

Dripping Taps. Other Red Flags that can easily be overlooked are leaking and dripping taps. Your viewers probably will assume that a dripping tap could be fixed with a new washer. If so, a ten cent washer will solve this problem. Get the washer and fix the problem before viewers have a chance to question it.

On the other hand, your viewers could quite easily think bigger and imagine that the consequence of a dripping tap is bound to be flooding, which leads to mold. If they start to visualize the grim possibility of having to tear out walls and calculate the high cost of repair and inconvenience, they will never make an offer.

Structural Defects. Look inside and outside for cracks in walls. Look for loose siding, damp spots, broken windows, flaking paint, crumbling steps, etc., all items that you should discuss with your inspector at the time of your pre-listing inspection. Take time to resolve any problems at the source rather than a superficial fix. Look inside your property for areas that show wear and tear. Try and see your house through the eyes of a buyer and *their* home inspector.

A great house close to a golf course had been on the market for months when I was brought in to stage it. With such a great location, the house should have sold in a heartbeat. The culprits were two small broken windows. Instead of replacing them, the homeowners had ignored them, telling themselves that if a potential buyer pointed them out, then the seller would negotiate the repair; after all it was just two small windows.

Wrong! Wrong! Wrong! If viewers were as cavalier about broken windows, the house would have been sold already. Instead, the viewers had been given a subliminal alert. They may have wondered if golf balls routinely fly through the windows and started worrying about their family's safety. One viewer said that they were concerned that the window may have been broken by vandals who had easy access to the property through the open golf course. None of those reasons were the case. In fact, a ladder had fallen and cracked the windows. It was one of the obvious problems the homeowner hadn't bothered to get around to. They felt the broken windows were too small to hassle with and totally inconsequential – and yet, when we repaired the windows (for $35 each), the house sold in two weeks.

In some homes that are slow to sell, I have actually seen wires hanging out of a wall. A viewer can't help but wonder, "Are those wires live?" Wires should never be hanging out of the wall. If your home has loose wires like this, investigate and ensure that the wires are capped properly.

In other houses, I've struggled with hard-to-open doors and come across peeling paint. It's astonishing. These are basic things that must be fixed. Sticking doors should be planed to allow free movement. Door locks, handles and hinges should be oiled to stop squeaks. Peeling paint should be scraped and replaced with a fresh new coat.

Wallpaper can also be a Red Flag. Most people hate stripping wallpaper and it seems to be a law of the universe that most people hate other people's wallpaper. So strip and paint. Get rid of borders. Those decorative wallpaper paper strips are terribly dated and a pain to take off.

A buyer's thoughts run rampant when they are touring your home. How do you know they aren't thinking, "Oh, no, all this wallpaper has to be stripped before that wall can be painted or re-wallpapered!" A buyer could be put off at the thought of having to rent a steamer and sweat over this unpleasant job.

Fix all structural defects before your viewers have a chance to let their minds take off in the wrong direction.

Examples of Red Flags

- Dirt and grime.
- Bad smells.
- Unkempt gardens/yards.
- Overgrown plants/flower beds.
- Unsafe and difficult-to-navigate driveways and pathways.
- Unclear property boundaries.
- *Autumn*: slippery, wet leaves.

- *Winter*: walkways and driveways blocked with ice and snow.
- Overgrown trees that block the view and the light into the house.
- Broken fences.
- Recycle bins and garbage bags (unless it is garbage pick-up day).
- Evidence of pets (messes, bones, hair, or toys).
- A dirty swimming pool.
- No house number visible from the street.
- Broken or dirty external light fixtures.
- Bland or dirty front door.
- Broken doorbell.
- Gutters and downspouts in poor repair or full of debris.
- Substandard surface: cracked and damaged walls, roof, siding, pathways, or driveways.
- Rotten window frames.
- Dried caulking on windows over 6-7 years of age.
- Torn screens.
- Dirty windows inside or out.
- Bug killers in view.
- Mouse traps or poisons in view.
- Peeling paint indoors or outdoors.
- Broken windows.
- Cracks in interior walls or foundation walls or in walkways.
- Damp spots.
- Mildew.
- Dirt and dust.
- Squeaky floorboards.
- Unsafe stair railings.
- Dripping taps.
- Wires hanging out of walls.
- Hard to open doors and drawers.
- Pets (especially cats, since so many people have allergies).
- Wallpaper.
- Bathroom plunger.

When black powder was noticed on a power outlet you could imagine the nightmare message it conveyed. Absolutely it meant a lost sale.

Your professional home inspector should be able to advise you on all of the above at the time of your pre-listing inspection. They will also be able to alert you to any other Red Flags that they would point out to potential purchasers if called to inspect this property.

When you are selling your home, you must make yourself acutely aware of all the Red Flags. Repair or attend to them before you list your home. Identifying a problem and ignoring it, or leaving a note, or telling a viewer that you will be

Black powder on a power outlet is a colossal Red Flag.

attending to the problem later, is too little, too late. Red Flags must be dealt with immediately. I cannot emphasize this more!

Sellers who ignore this step leave their home to Fixer-Upper buyers who represent only 10% of the market. By limiting themselves to these buyers, they will almost certainly take a serious hit on the price and significantly increase the time it takes to sell their home.

Taking down the Red Flags is no guarantee that your home will sell for a great price overnight, but it does give you the assurance that you've eliminated every problem you can anticipate. It should also give you the confidence to believe you can handle whatever comes along. If someone points out a new Red Flag, they can rest assured that you will handle it. Even before you sell your home, the confidence and gratification you'll gain makes the effort worthwhile.

TIPS: For reputable Home Inspection experts in Canada visit www.cahpi.com (Canadian Association of Home Inspectors), in Ontario www.phpio.ca (Professional Association of Home & Property Inspectors). In the UK visit www.rics.org (Royal Institute of Chartered Surveyors) and www.surveyorsweb.co.uk (Independent

Surveyors Association) and in the USA visit www.ashi.org (American Society of Home Inspectors).

Summary: Red Flags are the show-stoppers that will stall or prevent a sale. Pay attention to Red Flags. Attend to them before any showing. Buyers are super critical and will find every excuse to lower their offer. Leaving a note that the problem will be solved before the buyer takes possession is too little too late. Attending to the problem before it is discovered will prevent subliminal messages that may give doubt to other areas of the home. You need to give your buyer confidence that not only has this house has been well maintained, but it has been loved. Who wouldn't find a house like that inviting? In the long run these simple fixes will save you a considerable amount of money and anguish.

STEP TWO – CLUTTER

"I've been getting rid of some clutter
— anything that doesn't serve a positive purpose in my life —
and making room for things that feel happy to me."

~ Jan Denise

Clutter! Why do we hate it? Because clutter is VISUAL NOISE. Clutter confuses, distracts and muddles thought processes.

Why get rid of the clutter? Because you need your buyers' full attention. You only have about *nine minutes*. That's how long it typically takes for someone to tour your home. You must impress your buyers in that time.

You want them to imagine living in this house themselves. How can they do that, if your house is filled with distracting clutter? If they can't see past the encumbering clutter to the wonderful features of your home, then you are literally short changing yourself. If your house is buried in clutter, how can you expect them to appreciate the architectural jewels, such as crown molding, fireplaces, windows, doors, and floors? Part of the appeal of a new home is the enticing illusion that it represents a new, improved way of life. Even if they live in a cluttered house themselves, why would they want more of the same?

One of the complaints I hear all the time from homebuyers and realtors is that the interiors of some staged homes look unnatural. This raised my curiosity, so I investigated by going to look at these homes myself and I have to agree. Many of the staged homes I visited had been de-cluttered to the point of sterility. As a result, they felt uncomfortable and uninviting. I absolutely advocate that all clutter must be cleared out, but there is a fine line between sterile and stuffed. When the home is full of clutter, its charm and personality are buried. On the opposite end of the spectrum, however, a totally cleared out home feels unloved and barren. If done well, home staging brings out the best qualities in a home, without making it feel like a sterile showroom.

Clutter means different things to different people. Most homeowners recognize they have cluttered spaces, but they are unaware of its extent and don't really know how to address it.

Identifying and clearing clutter is usually an emotional and time consuming task. Few of us enjoy doing it. So, typically, it either doesn't get done or it gets overdone where everything, and I mean everything, is taken out. The key is to differentiate the good clutter from the bad clutter, then systematically categorize the clutter. This makes the job a whole lot easier.

How to Eliminate Clutter. First, look in and around your property with a critical eye. Just as you toured for Red Flags wearing your Black-Hat-of-Doom, you are now going to examine each area wearing a hypothetical Red-Hat-of-Emotion. Like it or not, clutter is emotional. Start with one room, any room, and focus your attention there.

You know what comes next. You are going to have to go through each item and make a decision: stay or go? Is it something you always think you're going to use, but never will? Or is it something you need and have genuinely been looking for, but couldn't find among the clutter? After that, if you keep it, you'll have to decide where to put it. (It's useless to you tossed in a pile like this.) But let's start with the questions that will let you make the basic cut.

If you can answer "yes" to any of these questions, get rid of it. Is this item...?

- Not regularly used?
- Not loved or cherished?
- Stored or left in the wrong place?
- A half-completed project you were meaning to finish?
- A broken object or appliance that cannot be used until it's fixed?
- An unwanted gift?
- A collection of disorganized artifacts that are unkempt, dusty, dirty, broken pieces or too large for available display space?
- A personal photograph collection displayed on walls or other surfaces?

Wait a minute, did I say, "Get rid of it"? A personal photograph collection? That project that you really do want to finish one day? How harsh!

It's a good idea to change your vocabulary, when it comes to sorting out your stuff. It's not so much about "getting rid of..." as "finding a new home for ..." When you come upon an item that causes you to answer one of these questions "yes", you can rest securely in the knowledge that you will be "finding a new home for it".

You would obviously never "get rid of" grandma's beautiful old teapot collection full of treasured memories. Even if it had been taking up the entire china cabinet in the dining room for more than a decade, while you've been keeping the china you use for formal occasions in a storage box in the garage, any suggestion that you should "get rid of" grandma's teapots would understandably meet with resistance. The phrase "finding a new home for" is softer and kinder and, frankly, more truthful.

I once saw a beautiful pair of white, Duncan Phyfe chairs at a yard sale, as I was driving home from work. I turned my car around in the street and went back. The husband standing on the lawn said they were $60 for the pair. I handed him the money immediately, just as his wife came out. When she heard the price, she was horrified. Her husband said, "Honey, they don't go with our stuff!" but she had tears in her eyes when she said, "I'm sorry, I can't possibly sell my grandmother's chairs." I told her, truthfully, "I will *love* these chairs. I know how wonderful they are." And she looked so relieved. She didn't really want them, but couldn't "get rid of them" either. Unless someone else would love them. Since then, I've always given away furniture I loved. It feels so much better to give it to someone who appreciates it than to make a few bucks.

Don't worry. We are not going to get rid of anything . . . Well, okay, technically, yes, some things. But more about that later. In the meantime, you're going to discover that finding a new home for all your unused items is very cathartic and liberating. Think of all the things you never used that could help other people or bring in some extra money. Feel the power! If you let yourself consider your most treasured items as "family", and you really cannot imagine living without them, then that feeling lets you know that those things are definitely keepers.

However, here's the deal: Less is more. If you must display grandma's teapots, select three or five of your favorites and display them on a single shelf of the china cabinet. Pack the rest carefully in boxes and store them until you reach your new home, then put the formal china that everyone will admire on display. A buyer will never have the good fortune of inheriting your grandma's teapots, but they may have great china of their own, so they'll be able to appreciate yours more easily.

Clutter Danger Zones. As you look further, be sure to check out the danger zones where clutter tends to accumulate. These zones will help you define the fine line between "good clutter" and "bad clutter." Judging from my experience in staging people's homes, I can say that the most *obvious* clutter is usually found in the following locations:

- On the front porch.
- In and around the garden and pathways.
- On steps and decks.
- In the foyer: on the stairs, over the newel post, or on the floor.
- On top, sides and door of refrigerator.
- On kitchen surfaces.
- On dining room tables and coffee tables.
- On the tops of desks and filing cabinets.
- Underneath desks (especially cabling or wires) on office floors.
- On the back of the toilet.
- On top of bathroom counter.
- In the shower or bath.
- On the top of nightstands.
- On any bedroom seating.
- On bedroom floors.
- Inside or on top of curio cabinets, bookshelves and shelving units.
- In the corners of the rooms.

Clutter that is contained and for the most part "out of sight" is known as the dreaded *hidden* clutter. It is important to be on the look out for this type of clutter, as well as the obvious clutter because potential buyers inevitably will find these hidden areas and look inside and underneath them. When they see all this stuff "out of sight," it can be as much of a turn off as seeing obvious clutter. In either case, clutter can negatively impact the sale.

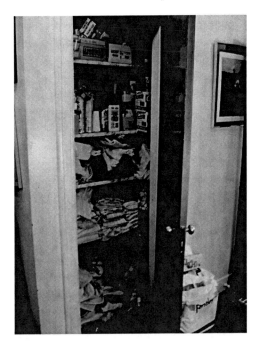

Warning: An overstuffed linen closet surreptitiously tells viewers that the house doesn't have enough storage space.

The point is you can't get away with hidden clutter. Not only will buyers mysteriously gravitate toward it, but it will contribute to the same kind of vaguely musty smell mentioned earlier. If your goal it to make your home feel clean and fresh, so your buyers can envision moving away from their own clutter, uncover all the hidden clutter you can find! As you move from room-to-room, area to area, look in these likely places for some of this familiar clutter – and anything else you can find that doesn't cast your home in its best light:

- Attics or crawl spaces, crammed with ragged boxes and broken toys.
- Basements, cluttered with tools, unused furniture and miscellaneous debris.
- Spare rooms, filled with dust, ironing boards and laundry.
- Garages, clogged with unfinished projects and remnants of all descriptions.
- Drawers bursting to the seams with crumpled clothes.

- Closets floors piled with shoes, handbags and fallen clothes.
- Refrigerators, smelly, overstocked or in disarray.
- Pantries, cupboards and cabinets, overfilled with old, half used, items that are past their best-before date.
- Junk drawers, cluttered with random objects.
- Under bed storage, collecting dust and clogging up the available space.
- Linen closets – stuffed, or poorly folded items which indicate the closet isn't big enough.
- Files or in-box trays, full of visible paper, mail, and documents.
- Magazine racks or stands with outdated magazines and newspapers.
- Multi-coloured flowers or bowls of mixed fruit that subliminally convey the message of clutter.

As much as possible, every area of your house should be free of all unnecessary heaps, collections, stacks or piles of things. A fresh, inviting home maintains the illusion of space in every way possible.

Cleaning out the clutter gives you another wonderful benefit: It frees your mind. Haven't you experienced the amazing sense of clarify and relief, after organizing a cupboard or eliminating a pile of debris from a corner. Along with the clutter goes your stress. One of the secondary benefits of staging your home is how much better it makes you feel as you see your house begin to shine!

> **TIPS: Fridge Clutter.** The only magnet on your fridge should be that of your real estate sales representative. Allow nothing else on the top, on the sides or on the door of your refrigerator.

Clutter-Free Exercise. Do you remember the black garbage bags, yellow garbage bags, cardboard boxes and plastic dollar store baskets I asked you to have on hand as part of your Toolkit? You have now arrived at the right time to use them. Now you can use these containers to create temporary new homes for your clutter in these 5 categories:

1) Keep and Display. Your treasured keep-and-display items are not really regarded as clutter. They are the pieces that reflect your happy, welcoming home. But again, less is more. Here's what to do: Select just 1, 3 or 5 beautiful or whimsical pieces from a collection. For example:

- Keep 1, 3 or 5 soft toys from your child's collection.
- Keep at least 2 of your kitchen small appliances (such as a toaster and coffee maker), if they can be polished to look fresh, sparkling and new.

You do want your home to look loved and lived in, not cold and sterile, so select pieces that reflect warmth and personality. Don't worry about where to display them for now. You will learn about that in *Step Seven – Finishing Touches*.

You will have things left over. Keep in mind that you are not eliminating them from your life. When you get into your new home, you can put as many of them on display as you'd like. For now, you are creating a special effect: You are staging your home. Pack the rest of the items in carefully labeled boxes, ready to open in your new home.

2) Put it into Storage. If you find that you have gone from the clutter of items, spread around your home, to the clutter of bags and boxes you need to keep them out of the way, renting a storage garage is the perfect solution. It is common to have items you will want to take out of your home for the duration of the sale to make your home spacious and clutter free.

- Search the internet for self-storage units. You will be amazed at how many there are in your area. The costs are usually competitive, reasonable and definitely worth the money. Check around for prices and sizes of garages, accessibility to your possessions, storage conditions and additional services. Using a storage garage is only an expensive idea if you are storing all your clutter only to have to deal with it at the other end all over again. It is not cost effective to store things that you will essentially never use.
- Make sure to get guarantees that your storage garage is clean, bug free, and – most importantly – dry. Some storage garages are individually contained units that are super secure, preventing a burglar from breaking in from another unit to steal your stuff.
- Consider storing things with friends and relatives. Assure them it will be only temporary.
- Select large boxes of the same size, and small boxes of the same size to make stacking easy. Make sure you put books and

other heavy items in the small boxes. Use your large boxes only for lighter items such as lampshades, bedding, etc.
- Do not store food or combustible products.

TIP: Pack non-essentials right away —they are the things that don't need to be dealt with at the last minute —and store them offsite. These boxes can consume a good deal of valuable room in your home and it's nicer to get them out of the way. Offsite storage units can hold boxes that don't need to be unpacked immediately after you've moved into your new house.

3) Sell it! It is almost a certainty that you have found items you are willing to part with, but believe you can sell. It would certainly be nice to get something back for them, if you can. Here are some solutions for selling:

- **Garage Sales** are a reliable method for selling second-hand items. Schedule it far enough in advance so that you can place a classified ad in the local paper. Try to pick a date on a non-holiday weekend, unless you live in a popular city or resort town with lots of tourists and holiday-makers. Remember, one person's junk is another's treasure. As you sift through your clutter and evaluate all the items in your house – inside and outside – identify with a sticker everything you want to sell. Take the time to scrub, wash, polish, dust and launder it. If it needs a simple repair that could greatly improve the price, fix it. As with staging your home, you will get more for your money if you spend some time fixing it up first.
- **Consignment Stores** are another way to trade cash for your possessions. Call each shop to get a clear idea about what type of things they buy. Make an appointment at the shops that you believe may be interested in your items. Ask a sales associate to explain the store's policies. Typically things are kept for a specific period of time. Sold items will earn you a portion of the selling price, whereas unsold items will be returned to you later, or donated to charity. Depending on the store, you may receive cash, credit or a cheque.
- **Online Auctions** allow participants to bid for products and services over the Internet. The world's largest online auction site is eBay; it has been so successful that many others sites

have copied their model. An auction site facilitates the process of listing and displaying goods, bidding on items, and paying for them. It acts as a marketplace for individuals and businesses that use the site to auction off goods and services. Check out *Kijiji* or *craigslist*. These online auction sites are localized which means you don't have to deal with shipping. Buyers will come and pick up the item.

- **Live Auction**. If you are downsizing and have lots and lots of high-quality items you would like to sell, you may want to consider an Auctioneer. Live auctions give you more flexibility than setting a fixed price and are less time-consuming and expensive than negotiating a price (as happens in a garage sale). In an auction competing bids are offered almost simultaneously. An auctionable item can be nearly anything – land, livestock, wine, flowers, fish, cars, furniture, tools, dishes, etc. Simply put, an auction is a method based upon competition. It is the purest of markets: a seller wishes to obtain as much money as possible, and a buyer wants to pay as little as necessary. Look in the yellow-pages or online to find an auctioneer near you.

TIP: Live Versus Online Auctions. The difference between a live auction and an online auction is simply the method in which the auction is brokered. A live auction happens at a specific location – usually an auction house or an estate, while an online auction takes place via the Internet.

Live auctions have the advantage of allowing the buyer to examine the goods for sale. Using reputable auction houses are less prone to fraud because the auction houses screen goods before they are sold.

The disadvantages of live auctions can be the distance to the site of the auction to participate, and holding a live auction can be costly to the seller.

Online auctions have the advantage of being available to people all over the world which helps to lower overall prices for both the buyer and seller. The disadvantage of online auctions is that you can't physically examine the goods for sale, and there can be the opportunity for fraud.

4) Donate it! If you have some things that are in great condition, but did not sell at the auction, would you be willing to donate to a worthy cause? Donating your unwanted possessions can be rewarding. There are several good options:

- Give your items to Charity Shops, Thrift Stores or Goodwill stores. If some items are too large for you to deliver, they will usually be happy to pick them up at an agreed-upon date. Beware the inspection of the thrift store worker, however. I have experienced a snub at the door when they did not consider my stuff to be quite up to thrift store standards. Select good stuff for them to pick up or you will be left holding the couch – as I once was. Also, be aware that charity shops have limited space for large appliances, couches, etc. They have become choosy because they have to pay for disposal of goods that don't sell.

- Enter "Charitable Organizations" or "Social and Human Service Organizations" into your favourite search engine for a list of groups who will happily take household products and clothes and recycle them within the community. There are many other charitable organizations that do not have a store front but welcome your second hand treasures. Be aware that some of the charity organizations will sell the items to a secondary service that turns the products into pulp for paper, or other products. If that disturbs you, then make sure you ask how they dispense of your items before pick up.

- Look in the yellow pages or on the internet for recycling organizations who will take your old computer equipment, phones, tires, etc.

5) Discard it! For absolutely everything that cannot be repaired or is completely worn out and really and truly considered junk, then put the discarded pieces to the curb, well before garbage day and often people will help themselves. I'd like to think that the discarded items could be re-purposed. But when even this idea has been exhausted, then make sure the pieces are back out there on garbage day. After all, *you gotta do what you gotta do.*

When you have large items or many black bags to dispose of at one time, call the city garbage collection department and ask that they pick up the bags of garbage at your curb. If the City Refuse Collection Department is forewarned about the large pickup most are happy to comply. Be prepared to make your own arrangements to take the items to the dump. The experience can even turn into an adventure. A City Refuse Collection worker once told me that he would bend the rule of five bags per household. He agreed to take as many bags as we could fling into the truck in five minutes! I gathered together a couple of friends and we took care of 68 bags in 4 minutes and 50 seconds flat! If you don't have the wherewithal or resources to take it to the dump yourself, you can call a residential garbage/recycling collection service who will either schedule a pick-up, or will drop off a skip for you to fill and for a fee they will haul it all away.

> **TIPS: Clutter.** Sort out your items into different coloured garbage bags. For example, use black bags for discarded items destined for the dump. Use Yellow bags for donated items intended for the charity shops. For storage containers, buy, or pick up a selection of large boxes of the same size and small boxes of the same size. It makes stacking so much easier. Put light items in large boxes, heavier items in small boxes. Print labels for the boxes, including your name, new address and phone number. Leave a few empty lines to list the contents of the box and another line to note the name of the room the box will end up in.
>
> It is hard to throw away your kids' artwork that is so proudly displayed on the fridge. To preserve their genius, stand your young artist by his or her work and take a photograph. The artwork can then either be discarded or the most precious pieces can go in a portfolio and dealt with at the new house. Display the photograph in their very own album. Better yet, give your children a huge boost in confidence and make them more proud than they can possibly be by matting and framing your child's most creative brilliance and displaying it on an empty wall. Art is in the eye of the beholder.

Summary: Clutter confuses, distracts and muddles the thought processes. It also presents subliminal messages that the house is not maintained. Minimize and simplify the home for your buyers, create the appearance of as much space as possible. Make it easy for buyers to imagine themselves living in this house.

STEP THREE – FOCAL POINTS

"Only one thing has to change for us to know
happiness in our lives: where we focus our attention."

~ *Greg Anderson*

Every room must have a focal point as the primary element that catches attention upon entering. Correctly chosen, the focal point will direct the eye to the benefits and features of your home. Poorly chosen, it exposes areas that you would sooner not highlight.

A good focal point gives the room a centre. It not only should capture your attention when you first walk in, it should also encourage you to take in and appreciate the rest of the room. You'll know you've decorated effectively around your focal point if the furnishings, lighting and accessories surrounding it are varied, yet balanced in such a way that your eyes rove around the room rhythmically (as opposed to randomly) and are eventually drawn back to the focal point.

A room's focal point should be something functional. In a bedroom, the obvious focal point is the bed. In a dining room, it's the table or chandelier. In a family room, it might be a fireplace or a widescreen television. Other examples might be a window with a beautiful view or an architectural feature. If the room has nothing going for it at all, then focus your buyer's attention on an impressive piece of framed artwork or a unique piece of furniture.

Your focal point will help determine the colour palette and types of materials that will be used throughout the room. It will guide the selection and placement of lighting, furnishings and upholstery. Permanent fixtures, as well as the room's furniture and accessories, should be proportionate to the room's focal point and arranged around it in a way that looks and feels balanced. You don't want a lopsided look, where one end of the room appears to be heavier than the other.

Spotlight attention on the focal point by clearing away any competing and distracting clutter and arrange furniture near the focal point so that it becomes the center of awareness in the room.

Every room needs a focal point – an object of concentrated or immediate attention. When staging a home, select one focal point for each room, it grounds the space and focuses your attention upon entering.

Focusing on a Fireplace. Whenever a fireplace is in a room, it is always the focal point. So it deserves special attention. If your room has a fireplace, make the most of it. Clean it thoroughly and polish any fire irons or surroundings. Draw attention to it by clearing the mantelpiece of accumulated paraphernalia. Arrange furniture around it, so that it becomes a welcoming, unmistakable centerpiece of the room.

A Beautiful View. A stunning view through a window could be a focal point. Emphasize it by framing the window lightly with drapery panels on either side. It might be enough to simply paint the window frame the same colour as the trim (baseboards, doorframes, etc.) and do without drapery altogether.

In a bay window, you may consider installing a built-in window-seat, or placing a single table in front of the window, or positioning a small, attractive, healthy plant on the ledge. It is important to arrange the furniture so the view isn't blocked by anything too large. Ideally, you want the window to be seen from all vantage points.

Gather furniture around a fireplace.

Furniture Focal Points. If your room does not have a fireplace or a beautiful view, establishing a focal point can be as simple as giving prominence to the largest piece of furniture in the room: a dining room table, an armoire, or a dresser. Any one of these pieces could be the focal point of a room. Whatever you choose for your focal point, make it count.

One of my clients' had a fabulous view of the gardens in her dining room. The room had a gorgeous black oak floor and copper-accented walls. Yet it was not the view, or the floor, or the walls that immediately caught your attention when you entered the room, it was the ugly brass chairs. We used a black matt spray paint on the brass to coordinate with the floors. Essentially this strategy helped the chairs blend in with the floor, so the focal point became the fabulous view.

Lighting. In a room with no redeeming architectural features, focus light on a stunning piece of artwork, position an uplight under a leafy plant to cast interesting shadows on the wall, or spotlight a sculpture on a pedestal. You can also use lighting to highlight crown molding, an interesting carved door, or to emphasize a stained glass window.

Walls. One way of establishing the focal point in a small room is to paint one wall a slightly darker colour from the rest of the room. We call this the "feature wall". This is best done on the wall facing you as you walk into the room. It will be the first thing people see, so it will give the room a feeling of greater size and depth.

Artwork or Sculptures. *Object d'art* can be highlighted on a pedestal or in an illuminated cabinet. A magnificent painting could be considered as the focal point. In a workout room, make the elliptical trainer the focal point by centering it in the room with smaller pieces of equipment around the room's perimeter. Use a magnificent mirror as your focal point, or a large painting positioned on the wall to draw attention.

Competing Focal Points. Many people have competing focal points, such as a television and a fireplace in the same room. Two focal points in a room will not work. If you have two focal points, you need to remove one of them.

When done correctly, a room is designed around its focal point. Chairs and tables are pulled into a cosy arrangement around a fireplace. Everything points to the mantle, which literally brings the room into focus. If there is a cosy arrangement of chairs around the mantle, but the other elements in the room – sofa, the coffee table, the rocking chair, the plants and the lighting – are centered around the television, it is like seeing a portrait with the eyes facing in opposite directions! When the focus is divided, the effect feels unnatural.

In the case of the television and fireplace, the architectural feature is the fireplace, so unless it is an electric portable unit, the fireplace wins every time. The television should be moved to another room or out of the house entirely. Nonetheless, in my experience, this is almost impossible for most homeowners to agree to. Look at it this way; you are re-defining the purpose of the room. Your living room is now a conversation area. The television can be moved to another room in the home that needs a focal point or be moved out of the home altogether.

It's the same scenario for a bedroom. The bed is usually the focal point, but with a television in the corner, you have two focal points. The television has to be temporarily relocated. Remember, this is only for the duration of the sale. The television can come back into that room as soon as the sale is finalized.

Summary: *Give every room one focal point. It is the primary element that focuses your attention upon entering. It gives the room a centre and brings unrelated elements together. Clear away clutter to showcase your focus and arrange furniture or accessories around to further display the piece. Once you have your focal point, everything else tends to fall into place.*

STEP FOUR – COLOUR

*"My choice of colours does not rest on
any scientific theory; it is based on observation, on feeling,
on the very nature of each experience."*

~ Matisse

Colour is a very personal matter. Everyone brings their own associations to different shades. Lavender wall paint in a bedroom may bring back warm memories of their childhood home to one person and do absolutely nothing for another. A daisy-yellow kitchen may make you smile every time you walk into the room, but a potential buyer may prefer grey-blue.

In this section you will learn how to select a colour that appeals to the majority of people. When it comes to selling a house, how and where colour is applied is a critical choice in making or breaking a sale.

Colour is of primary importance in every design; it can alter a room's mood and affect the perception of space and light in the room. It can change the way a room "feels" without changing its dimensions in the least. It can create illusions of height, width, warmth, spaciousness, cosiness, relaxation and contentment.

Many staged homes I have seen have been freshly painted in a nice safe beige colour. There is nothing wrong with painting walls this colour, except that it's become such a trend that there is now a sea of beige homes for sale. They all look alike. It seems that somehow *beige* is interpreted as a *neutral* – an ambiguous colour that everyone will like. Did you know that there are literally thousands of neutrals that are not beige? Beige is nice. But you don't want people to say your house is "nice." You want them to say, "Wow!" By using exactly the right neutral that is not beige, you can make your home stand out from all the others.

I have used a *neutral* blue, green, pink, or peach colour in every one of the homes I have staged for sale. Every one of these staged homes has sold within three to four weeks. So don't let anyone tell you that if you apply colour you reduce your chances of a sale. It is what is selected and where it is applied that makes or breaks the sale. The secret is to use a *muted* colour which is also referred to as a neutral. More about that later in this chapter.

How Colour Works. Before we launch into a discussion of how to choose colour for your home, it is important to delve a little into the history and psychology of colour to understand how it all works.

Colour is how our eyes and brain interpret light. In 1790, researcher Thomas Young said the human eye sees only three colours: red, blue, and yellow. They are called the primary colours. They are the three lowest common denominators and none of them can be made by combining the others. For instance, mixing red and yellow together will not make blue.

Secondary colours are created by mixing the primary colours. Red and yellow make orange. Blue and red make purple. Yellow and blue make green. Sir Isaac Newton famously listed the primary and secondary colours in the sequence we see in the colours of the rainbow: red, orange, yellow, green, blue, indigo, and violet. He then arranged the colours in a circle which he named *The Colour Wheel*. This is a very useful tool. Designed in the 17th Century is still used to this day to help decorators and artists interpret and mix colours.

We have been talking about primary and secondary colours; did you think I had forgotten about black and white? Sorry to disappoint, but black and white are not colours; they are shades and tints. When black and white are mixed in with the colours, they represent all the possible colours the human eye can process. Amazing, isn't it?

- When black is mixed with a colour it becomes darker. For example if black were mixed with red then we would have a dark shade of red.
- When black and white are mixed together the result is grey. If we mix in a little grey to our red, we will get a medium red.
- When white is mixed with red we would get a light red (pink).

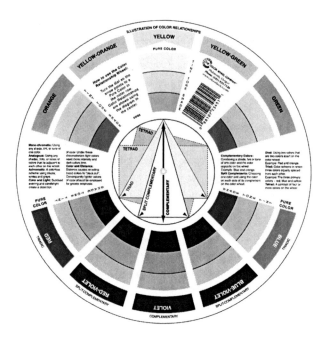

The Colour Wheel.

Now here is the biggest revelation of all: We, the human race, instinctively and unconsciously demand a balance of the three primary colours for our well-being, comfort and contentment. When a room doesn't feel comfortable or welcoming, it is often because the balance of colours is out of kilter. This is why choosing colour for a resale home is so vitally important – get a balance of the three primary colours and you will attract far more buyers. Forget one of the colours and you will propel the buyer out of the door.

Earlier I talked about the colour beige being understood as the only neutral. Beige is an equal mixture of the three primary colours, as well as black and white. So what is wrong with beige? Nothing! But there are literally thousands of neutrals that are not beige and they are the colours that say "Wow!" and set your home apart from the others.

Recognizing a neutral colour takes some study. The all-important neutral colour perfect for home staging consists of a base colour – say, blue – with small quantities of its complementary colour. For example, if you look at The Colour Wheel, you can turn the dial to find that the complementary colour of blue is orange. Even the smallest possible amount of orange will subdue blue, giving it a muted look, otherwise known as a neutral blue.

The same works for green. Equal quantities of blue and yellow mixed together give us a pure, clear shade of green. For it to be seen as a neutral green, the pure green must contain some of its complementary colour: red. It is the red that subdues the brightness of the green and make it more pleasing to the human eye.

And to really bring this home, let's take the colour yellow. Pure bright yellow on the walls definitely would be difficult to take for most people. But if you really like yellow and want to put it on your walls, you would instead use a neutral yellow. This is a pure yellow that has a little of its complementary colour added: purple (which is blue and red mixed together). A tiny amount of purple will subdue bright yellow, making it far more comfortable to live with.

Can you see what happened here? The three primary colours were used to create three perfect neutrals! Now I know you are not going off to the paint store to mix your own paint colours – that would be a ridiculous thought. No, what you are doing is learning to distinguish the muted colour from the pure colour. The muted colours are what we want to use to stage a house.

Imagine! The tens of thousands of colours in all the various paint colour decks are made from the three primary colours and black and white!

So how many colours does the human eye see? Scientific experiments have shown that humans can discriminate between very subtle differences in colour and estimates the number of colours we can see, range as high as ten million.

Wait a minute! We are expected to select colours for our home that will be pleasing to the largest possible audience – and we have ten million colours to choose from? It is no wonder that the old standby beige is there to rescue us. If you want your home to stand apart from the others look for neutral colours. *You can learn more about what colours to use by visiting my website, www.spotlightondecor.com.*

Decorators and Designers learn the intricacies of The Colour Wheel during their studies and use these techniques when selecting colour for their clients. You can use this tool too, to select colours when you are ready to sell your home. There's more... on the Colour Relationships side of the wheel that we'll be working on, you will find the secrets of making colour choices for the *moods* you wish to convey. This nifty tool is perfect to help you choose the right mood for your home.

Here are some of the key terms from The Colour Wheel that we will be using to help pick the perfect colour for your walls or accessories.

Monochromatic values allow you to create many variations from a single colour by adding black, grey or white. For staging a home, we will be selecting three Monochromatic values to establish continuity throughout. Monochromatic values are often called a *family* of colours. They link areas and provide flow from room to room, so when you want an area to be interesting and appealing you would use monochromatic values on your walls, doors and trim. You will learn how to use monochromatic values later in *Step Two: Selecting Your Wall Colours.*

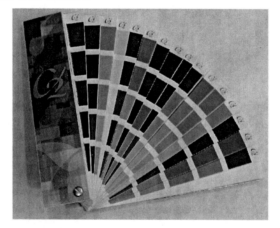

A variety of monochromatic values can be found in a Paint Deck.

Analogous colours sit next to each other on The Colour Wheel. They tend to look pleasing together because they are closely related. Yellow, yellow-orange, and orange are an example of analogous colours. They blend perfectly in *Sunflowers*, a painting by Vincent Van Gogh. How do you know that these colours are closely related? They each share the colour yellow.

Sunflowers by Vincent Van Gogh.

We select Analogous accessories to add harmony to a room. Analogous colours are in agreement with each other. They are calming and pleasing to the eye. When you want a room to be calming and tranquil, choose accessories in analogous colours.

> **TIP: Try This.** Select a primary colour and a secondary colour. For example, you might choose blue and green. They look pleasing together because they are similar; they sit side-by-side on the colour wheel. They are analogous. With these two colours alone, you can create even more analogous colours — blue-green and purple and lots of others in between. All of these will have a colour in common: blue.

Complementary Colours complete each other. Placing two colours together that are complementary makes each appear much stronger. The complementary pairs are red-green, blue-orange and yellow-violet.

> **TIP: Try This.** To find a complementary colour, stare at a single colour (red, for example) for thirty seconds. Then look at a white surface. An afterimage of the complementary colour will appear. If you stare at red, the complementary image will always be green. If

you stare at the colour blue, the complementary image will be orange, and yellow will produce a purple after-image.

Complementary colours create excitement and contrast when they appear together. So we select accessories in complementary colours to add vibrancy and pizzazz to a room. When these complementary colours are placed together, they tend to looked balanced. Each colour even appears brighter. Complementary colours are colours that are flattering to one another. The dynamic tension between them is energetic. When you want a room to feel vibrant and alive, add complementary accessories. Toss a yellow cashmere throw over the arm of a deep purple sofa. Arrange a bouquet of bright orange starburst lilies in a royal blue vase. You'll immediately notice the excitement it creates.

Warm Colours are primarily considered to be red, orange and yellow. This colour family is called "warm" because it evokes warmth by association with flames – the sun, a torch, a fire. Warm colours have such a strong effect that they can even make you become warmer because the colours themselves affect your nervous system directly. Amazing as it seems, they can noticeably increase your circulation and body temperature!

Warm colours are also advancing colours. In other words, they appear to come toward you. In a selection of colours from across the spectrum, these are the colours you see first. That is why warning and hazard signs are red, orange and yellow. We have red traffic lights, stop signs, and fire engines. Red signifies passion, anger, the Devil and Cupid. Because it is so stimulating, red is the colour most commonly found in national flags.

In the theatre, the colours red and yellow on the set are used very carefully. They are used only to draw the eye to that part of the stage that has some importance. Actors who are dressed in red or yellow typically have some importance to the performance. Your eye is drawn to those characters first. Likewise in your home, only use these advancing colours to draw the eye toward a feature of the home you want your buyers to notice. A painting with red accents positioned on the wall over a fireplace will draw the eye to the mantle and surround. A beautiful granite kitchen island would be accented with a bowl of lemons or red apples to draw the eye to this feature.

Warm colours can work wonders in a room that doesn't get any sunlight. In a north-facing room, warm up the room by using paint colours in a muted creamy yellow or muted peach. Warm colours tend to create an illusion of bringing the walls in, which makes the room appear inviting, friendly and cosy. Dark, warm colours look dramatic. If the colour is painted at the end of a long narrow room, the room will appear to be shorter. So when you want to create a friendly and welcoming room, always use warm colours.

Cool Colours are in the blue, green and purple families. This colour family is called "cool" because it suggests coldness by association with water, ice, mountains, heather and the sky. Cool colours recede into the background.

Light, cool colours create the illusion of spaciousness. Painting the walls of a room in cool colours makes the room feel more open and refreshing – a very welcome effect in a south-facing room with a lot of sunlight. Because it is soothing, blue is a psychologically influential colour. Because we feel good when we are calm, most people cite blue as their favourite colour. The cool, calming effect of blue creates relaxation and makes time pass more quickly and it can help you sleep. Blue is an especially good colour for bedrooms.

Select predominantly cool colours in a south-facing room which gets warm in the sun. One of my south-facing homes had a Wedgwood-blue (which is a muted blue) entryway and a white floor tile with ribbons of grey-blue marbled throughout. The colour appealed to buyers, it did not deter them. The house was sold in 2 weeks.

When you want to give the illusion of the room being open and airy, go for cool colours, such as light muted blues, soft muted blue-greens, and delicate muted lavenders.

What You Should Know about Green. It is worth taking a minute to direct our attention to the colour Green. This is the colour in the centre of the rainbow. It is a mixture of a warm colour (yellow) and a cool colour (blue), which means that if it is mixed with slightly more yellow than blue, it will be a warm green. If it is mixed with more blue than yellow, it will be cool green. Green is the most relaxing colour to the human eye. Add a little of its complementary colour, red, and you get the most beautiful muted greens.

A very light, muted green is an appealing paint colour when preparing a home for sale. It contains each of the primary colours, red, blue and yellow. Teamed with an analogous colour to maintain harmony, or a complementary colour to add vibrancy, muted-green is always successful. The very first house I sold had soft muted-green walls with matching draperies and parquet flooring. I painted the feature wall a slightly darker muted-green. I then found four toss cushions to match that colour for my cream-coloured sofa.

The first people to walk though the door were so enthusiastic that they wanted me to leave the furniture and drapery.

It is a good idea to place green plants in all the major rooms – such as living room, dining room, kitchen and bathroom – to give the rooms a powerful jolt of energy and life. Just looking at a green plant on the desk beside your computer will give your eyes a rest when you have been staring at a computer monitor for a long time. What do you do when you have a room with no windows, or you don't have a green thumb, or you are unable to attend to keeping real plants alive? It is quite acceptable to buy or rent good quality silk plants for your staging. The foliage on silk plants today is so real looking that they could fool the most sophisticated horticulturist. But I am getting ahead of myself. I have devoted a whole section to accessorizing in *Step Seven, the Finishing Touches.*

Three-Step Colour Selection. When it comes to colour, this is the burning question of the day: "What exactly is the right colour that appeals to the majority of people which would help them imagine themselves living in my home?"

The Three-Step Colour Selection will help you create the perfect colour scheme for your home. Whether you plan to keep your existing wall colour – and add analogous coloured accessories for harmony or add complementary coloured accessories for vibrancy and pizzazz – or whether you plan to change the paint colour based on your existing accessories the effect will be amazing.

I'll let you in on a secret: This Three-Step Colour Selection is not just for home staging. You can use this technique to choose the perfect colours for your new home!

Step One: *Finding Your Inspiration.* Start by choosing one key object as your *Inspiration* which will help you find exactly the right colour. Turn your attention to fixtures in the room that you love and are in great shape and that are also the things that cannot be changed easily; for example, the hardwood floor or the carpets, or the countertops. But, if you are changing the floor, or replacing the countertops, then turn your attention to another source. Look for an object such as sofa, rug or artwork. Since size doesn't matter, it could be as small as a colourful button or a pebble.

In one of my homes, I picked the colours from my chinaware. The dishes were white with muted green and yellow squares around the rim. I painted the kitchen in a lighter tint of the same green and the dining room in a lighter tint of the same yellow. Then I set the table with my chinaware. The finished look was spectacular. The house sold in less than 3 weeks.

If you have exhausted that avenue and still don't feel inspired, look in your closet. What's the predominate colour you are most comfortable wearing? If you like it enough to wear it all the time, it will make an excellent choice as the basis of your colour scheme.

I took a client through this exercise when we were redecorating her home. When we looked at the floor, wall, countertop, sofa, and artwork options, we realized we would be replacing all those items, so they couldn't be the inspiration of the colour scheme. As a last resort, we looked for inspiration in her wardrobe. My client, Marianne, had lost a lot of weight recently and was in the market for a personal new look, so – again – all of these colours were likely to change! It appeared we had exhausted all our options.

As we sipped our tea and thought it over, Marianne started talking wistfully about her last vacation. I was caught up in the imagery of her memories as she described her holiday on a tropical island – collecting pastel-coloured seashells under swaying coconut palms and wiggling her toes in the soft, white sand of an endless beach.

Seashells used for Inspiration.

This idyllic place was Sanibel Island in Florida. I asked her to select her favourite shells from among those she had carefully assembled in a beautiful shadow box. We scrutinized their colours and found creams, blues, burgundies and soft greys. One little seashell created the colour scheme for her entire apartment. Nature doesn't make mistakes when it comes to integrating colours in objects, so selecting something from nature was a huge success.

Once you have determined your Inspiration, it is time to move to the second step.

Step Two: *Selecting Your Wall Colour.* (If you are satisfied with your clean, painted walls, then this step can be skipped, and you can move onto Step Three.) When you are looking for a colour for your walls, use your colour deck (see *Chapter 6: Tools of the Trade*) to find the one colour that most closely matches a colour in your Inspiration. There is always one colour in your inspiration that stands out for you and creates most appeal. In your colour deck, above and below your selected colour, you will see the same colour in varying intensities; these are your **Monochromatic values.** The 'family' of colours. From the same family, select three colours, all adjacent to each other, a light, medium and darker shade. These will be the colours for your walls.

Using these three colours throughout the visible areas of the house will create continuity and flow. Notice I said the *visible areas* of the house. These are the areas that can be seen as you travel from the hallway, through to the kitchen and dining room, through to the living room and any other room that is adjacent to the living areas, such as the stairs, landing and upper hallway.

To continue the illusion of continuity, the secret is to make sure that the window frames, door frames, both sides of the doors and baseboards are painted the same colour throughout the entire house. This is what establishes a connection from one room to another. The colour to use should be a creamy white which looks expensive. I don't recommend using a blue white when staging, it looks too stark. The colour you select to create the illusion of continuity must be chameleon-like to combine perfectly with both warm and cool colours. A good choice would be Benjamin Moore's Cloud White CC-40, or Pratt & Lambert's Designer White 33-1. Both these colours take on the hue of warm and cool colours and look rich and luxurious. To be absolutely sure, ask in your favourite paint store for a white that will work well with your chosen paint 'family'.

The bedrooms and bathrooms are considered the private rooms in the house where the doors are closed most of the time, so these are the rooms in which you can present some gentle creativity. In the bedroom you can select your favourite colour from the bedspread, and from there, in the colour deck, you will find the three monochromatic colours of the same family. In the bathroom, you can select three monochromatic colours using inspiration from your vanity top, wall or floor tiles.

Where to Use the Colours

- Use the trim colour on all window frames, door frames, both sides of the doors and baseboards throughout the entire house.
- Use the light and medium monochromatic colours interchangeably on the walls of the visible areas.
- Use the slightly darker shade as a distinctive feature colour to give some areas of your home added importance. Special areas receiving this treatment might be the wall that faces you when you walk into the room, on the inside of archways and passthroughs, or on walls on which there is a fireplace mantle. Used sparingly, the feature colour will add depth, interest and style.

Step Three: Selecting the Perfect Colour Accessories. Accessories can make or break your home staging, so I have included a whole chapter devoted to the finishing touches. But before you get there, let's talk briefly about creating a mood.

If your room hungers for tranquility, relaxation and calmness, the perfect accessory colours can be found in the Analogous palette.

If you want your room to be sizzling with vitality, vibrancy and pizzazz, then your perfect accessory colours can be found in the Complementary palette.

These moods will create a balanced personality that everyone will enjoy. Be careful; use one or the other; Analogous or Complementary colours – never both together.

TIPS: Working with Colour. Most potential buyers are attracted to light colours. If you stick with light, muted colours and minimal patterns, you will also create illusion of space.

- Paint ceilings white to make the room feel taller.
- Some people ask if they should add a little wall colour to the white ceiling paint. When staging your home, keep it simple and stay with the white only.

- Trim – that is, baseboards, door frames, doors and window frames – should be painted with the same colour throughout your home to convey continuity and flow. Every designer has their favourite white, mine is Benjamin Moore's Cloud White. I call this a chameleon white because it works well with every other colour."
- Use the darker Monochromatic colour for an accent wall to serve as a focal point wall.
- A disproportionately long room can be made to look shorter by painting the one end a deeper or a warmer colour.
- To make a room look bigger use light, cool colours on the walls and floors.
- Repaint over strong colour schemes. Defining areas, using monochromatic differences in depth of colour, can create a visual division in the room.

Optical Illusions: light and cool colours will expand a room or raise a ceiling, whereas dark and warm colours will appear to reduce a room's size and lower a ceiling.

Paint: It is worth spending more money for quality paint. Resist buying the cheap stuff. Good-quality paints cost more because they have a higher covering ability and increased durability. The high-end paints go on more smoothly, splatter less, and are fade resistant. Look for paint with low VOC (Volatile Organic Compounds), because it will have fewer odours than regular paints.

Be particular with the finishing sheen you select. *Sheen* refers to the degree of shine. Flat paint is recommended for ceilings, but is not such a good choice for walls in high-traffic areas. Eggshell works well in bedrooms, dining rooms and living rooms where frequent cleaning is not needed. Satin is a good choice for hallways, bathrooms, kitchens and children's rooms, and semi-gloss paints are a good choice for trim, doors, and baseboards since they are easier to wash. Only use high-gloss paints for trim, cabinetry, and doors in perfect condition.

If you are painting the rooms yourself, be sure to use the right equipment. Choose brushes with long, dense bristles: nylon for latex (water-based) paint and natural fibers for oil-based paint. A 2-inch, angled sash brush, a 3-inch trim brush, and good quality rollers are enough for most jobs. For rough or textured surfaces, get a roller with a 3/8-inch or thicker nap; for smooth surfaces, use a roller with a nap of 1/4 to 3/8 inch.

Never skip the prep work. Remove switch plates and other hardware. Fill in holes with spackling compound. Scrape off any flaking paint and sand the walls. Wipe off sanding dust and wash dirty walls with a TSP (trisodium phosphate) solution and rinse with plenty of clean water. Apply a primer to help conceal stains and ensure uniform colour. Paint covers more uniformly on a clean, dry, non-glossy surface. It is a nice touch to label the used paint cans with the colour number, the room in which it was used and the date, then store the cans in a dry place for the future owner. In addition, write the paint details on the backside of a switch plate in the room in which the paint was used.

Summary: How colour is applied is critical to making or breaking a sale. We, the human race, instinctively and unconsciously demand a balance of cool and warm colours for our well-being, comfort and contentment. Use your colour wheel to help make wise decisions. Creatively applied, colour can change the way a room 'feels' without changing its dimensions in the least. In general, light and cool colours will expand a room or raise a ceiling. Think continuity from room-to-room. It's always good to have one or two rooms that are totally unique and personal; as a rule, those rooms are reserved for the bedroom or bathroom.

STEP FIVE – LIGHTING

*"There is no more worthy, more glorious or
more potent work, than to work with light."*

Omraam Mikhaël Aïvanhov

Next to colour, lighting is arguably one of the most important elements when staging a home. In this section you will learn theatrical secrets for highlighting areas you want your buyers to notice. Light gives life to a room and is instrumental in setting the mood. Sales and marketing people have known for years that there is a curious psychological link between the quality of light and the emotions it creates. Lighting can convey warmth and intimacy. It can create the right atmosphere for entertaining or for working on a task. And with global warming, people are more conscious of what they plug in the wall.

Selecting a light fixture is just the beginning. You must also think about how many lamps you need, where will they need to be placed, what sort of light bulbs are best, where will you use a dimmer switch and how will you create illusions with lighting to change a room's size, height and width? These are all questions you will be able answer after reading this section.

Warm light has a yellowish-pink cast. Warm light conveys feelings of security, comfort, and relaxation – all the qualities your potential buyers want in a new home. It is also preferred for living spaces because it is more flattering to skin tones and clothing. Use warm light in living room, dining room, bedroom & bathroom spaces. Look for a soft white light bulb.

Cool light has a bluish cast. Cool light is preferred for visual tasks because it produces higher contrast than warm light. Use cool light in the kitchen, laundry room, and office for task lighting. Look for white daylight bulbs for the crisp, bright natural light that is so great for workshops, laundry rooms, etc.

Five Types of Lighting. To ensure that you get the best effect for your rooms, it is important that you first understand the five types of home lighting. We use a variety of lighting sources on the stage. They add interest, intrigue and variety. The same goes for your home. Using a mixture of interior lighting sources in a room is highly desirable and will create very dramatic effects. It is important to give a good overall lighting with natural light and overhead lighting. There should be lighting over work areas, reading areas and play areas. Focused lighting brings the eye to the home's architectural gems. When staging your home, be sure that every light fixture has the maximum allowable wattage.

Ambient, or general lighting, illuminates the whole room. This is the light that is soft and indirect, such as the ceiling fixtures you use on a regular basis. If you have a chandelier, recessed pot lights or track lighting, they are also considered general lighting. Ambient light creates just enough light for you to do general everyday jobs and to illuminate your route to the refrigerator in the middle of the night. Ambient decorative lights are adorning elements in the space itself. Chandeliers are ambient lights that can be installed in a hallway, a dining room, over a bathtub or at the end of a bed. Make sure every room has good ambient lighting.

Task lighting, as the term suggests, helps you perform the task at hand, such as reading, cooking, shaving, etc. Task lighting comes in many forms. It can include under-the-counter lighting in the kitchen, floor lamps, table lamps, bedside lamps, bathroom mirror lights and workshop adjustable lamps. Task lighting should be glare free and make things easy to see without tiring your eyes. Be aware that halogen bulbs generate a very stark white light. Task lights that use fluorescent bulbs can also be hard on the eyes. Whenever you use a task light, be sure to have other lights on in the room to reduce the strain on your eyes.

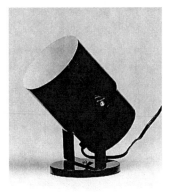

Accent lighting creates a mood and adds interest to a room by highlighting certain areas or objects, such as artwork, plants, and architectural elements in a room. Usually about three times brighter than ambient lighting, accent lighting is also known as "spotlighting." Examples of accent lights might be a bright ceiling pot-light or track light, angled to illuminate your subject; a light in a cabinet or alcove to display its contents; or a decorative light with a

An Uplight

lampshade, suspended over a kitchen island.

One of my favourite accent lights is the "uplight." Placing an uplight in a gloomy corner, below a leafy plant can create interesting shadows, lighten a dark corner and make the room appear larger. Experiment with lighting a wall, even when there is not an object to spotlight. Streaks of light can create visual interest in an otherwise blank space.

Natural light comes from the sun. It can flood in through windows, doors, and skylights, providing you are not blocking that daylight with heavy window dressings or furniture. Depending on the directional aspect, the time of day, season, or weather, the light can vary in brightness and intensity. Window draperies, sheers, blinds, or shutters should be made adjustable to control the natural light in a room.

Coloured glass transoms, crystals or even prisms can beautifully reflect natural iridescent light into the room. Amplifying the natural glow of the light as it changes throughout the day can enhance the atmosphere in rooms that receive the most light.

Candlelight, it is said, is the kindest light to a woman's complexion. No doubt a man's too. Lit candles elicit beautiful emotions, but to have lit candles in a staged home while viewers journey through the house is not a safe, sensible idea so I don't recommend it. If you have candles that have been used, get rid of them. If the candles have never been lit but are faded or dusty, then get rid of them, too. Pack up in boxes all the other candles for your new home. But be not candle-less. In recent years there has been a revolutionizing advancement: the LED (light emitting diode) candle.

I just love the LED battery-operated, faux candles which provide a very realistic, soft flickering light. They come in lots of colours and sizes with details like wicks that look like they have been burned and some have real wax surfaces. You can find them at most home-accent stores.

Create memory makers for your viewers by using them where you want to add just a touch of warm light to an interior display. Tuck faux candles into displays in bookcases. Use them in the fireplace in the summer for a delightful flickering display. Read more ideas for the fireplace in *Step Seven, Finishing Touches.*

The New Fangled Illuminations. Lighting has become complicated over the past few years. With global warming, our attention has been drawn to the many other alternatives to lighting our homes. Incandescent light bulbs are gradually being replaced by CFLs (Compact Fluorescent Light bulbs), LEDs, and other devices, all of which offer more visible light for the same amount of electrical energy input.

The incandescent lamp has been around since the 1800's and is widely used in household and commercial lighting. It has a low manufacturing cost, but it creates heat when running, thereby using a lot of electricity. The new CFLs and LEDs run cool to the touch and use less electricity. Some government authorities are endeavouring to ban the use of incandescent light bulbs in favour of more energy-efficient lighting. In some countries around the world, this has already been announced.

The energy saving CFLs are fast replacing the standard incandescent light bulbs. Ireland will stop using incandescent bulbs by January 2009. Australia has announced that by 2010, incandescent light bulbs will be banned, making it the first country in the world to announce such a ban. In Canada, the Ontario Government announced that it is planning to ban the sale of inefficient lighting in 2012.

Gone are the days when we would replace a 100-watt light bulb without a second thought. Today, this simple task has us standing in front of an array of curious looking light bulbs, displayed in packages that attempt to educate us with their perplexing terminology and entice us with their exotic shapes. We are left wondering just how super-ugly the chandelier over our dining room table will look with the new curlicue light bulbs. It is easy to imagine that the complexions of our dinner guests are likely to resemble those of lizards, and that the colour of our food will drive us from the table!

Still, there are more plusses than minuses for using CFLs. They do use less power and have a longer rated life (though they generally have a higher purchase price as of this date). They save electricity costs and can save 2000 times their own weight in greenhouse gases, but they do contain mercury, a poisonous heavy metal which complicates their disposal.

The really good news is that aesthetically, many are starting to look familiar with attractive shapes similar to that of the incandescent light bulb. The "soft white" CFLs are subjectively similar in colour to standard incandescent lamps.

Be aware that the CFL light bulbs do take a few minutes to "warm up." The lights start off looking gloomy, but within a short time, they reach their maximum brilliance. Some viewers poke their heads in a room, switch on the light, then, within seconds, they are off to the next room. This practice does not allow the lights to reach their full potential. For that reason, *make sure all lights are switched on* before a potential buyer comes to view your home.

Effective Lighting Techniques. As you assess each room for appropriate lighting, begin by considering the activities taking place in these rooms and the look you are trying to achieve. Count the number of light sources in the area. To really make your home stand out, you will want to use multiple types of lighting. This is called "layering." By using at least five different lighting sources in each room, you will add interest, versatility and, in some cases, very dramatic effects.

There are literally thousands of different light bulbs on the market from incandescent, compact fluorescent, halogen, LED, and then there are frosted, clear, crystal and coloured bulbs. How on earth do you pick the right one?

The first rule of thumb is to select the highest wattage allowable for your light fixture when staging a home. Install dimmer switches wherever you can, but, make sure that the light bulb you are dimming is compatible with a dimmer switch. Many are not. Clear glass light fixtures should have clear bulbs installed. Fixtures with enclosed shades should have the frosted bulbs. Outdoor porch lights or chandeliers should have clear or crystal light bulbs.

Specific Room Lighting Ideas. When you are in a room checking the lighting sources, try to make sure you have at least three of the five sources of light – preferably all five in each area. If there is a special light fixture that you will be taking with you to your new place, then replace it with a new one before your viewers set their hearts on it too. Don't be tempted to replace it with the old chandelier you took down and kept in the basement. (If you didn't like it, why do you suppose your buyer would?)

Minimum Lighting Fixtures

- Kitchens: Overhead, task, under-counter, recessed, pendant and natural light.
- Dining Rooms: Chandelier, pendant, wall washer, candlelight and natural light.

- Bedrooms: Table lamps on bedside tables, overhead light, closet light, accent light and natural light (For children's rooms, avoid halogen lamps, which can get very hot.)
- Bathrooms: moisture-proof pot-lights above the shower, bathtub and sink; shadow-free fluorescent or incandescent lights around mirrors and; nightlights.

TIPS: Working with Lighting

- Installing your lighting on a dimmer switch is convenient to give flexibility in creating the right mood, but be aware than some compact fluorescent lamps (CFLs) do not take kindly to the dimmer switch. Be sure to check the packaging.
- Make a narrow room look wider by washing one wall with light to visually expand it.
- Lower a high ceiling and make the room more intimate and cosy, by not allowing the light to escape beyond the height of a portable floor or table light/lamp shade.
- Make a small room look larger with uplighting on the ceiling.
- Vary the height of lamps to provide interest. Use table lamps around the outside edges of the room on shelves and tables. They'll radiate light inward, making the room feel spacious, yet cosy.
- Provide good general lighting without being too bright (uplight or downlight) by using wall sconces.
- Position a freestanding uplight or floor lamp behind the sofa.
- Mount wall lights beside features that won't be moving, such as an alcove or a fireplace.
- Place a light to one side, behind or above a chair.
- Make sure every light bulb is to its maximum wattage in the light fixture and it is clean, and in working order. When multiples (such as chandelier lights, vanity lights, etc.) are together be sure they match in size, shape and intensity.
- Open up the blinds and drapes, then keep the windows sparkling clean to let in as much light as possible.
- CFL light bulbs take a few minutes to "warm up." Make sure all lights are switched on before a potential buyer comes to view your home.

The Seductive Power of Home Staging

Summary: Lighting is instrumental in setting the mood of any room. Focus on functional and aesthetic light sources. Using all five lighting types in a room is highly desirable and will create very dramatic effects. Lighting can also be helpful in creating the illusion of changing a room size, height and width.

STEP SIX – SPACE PLANNING

"When I look down, I miss all the good stuff.
When I look up, I just trip over things."

~ Ani Difranco

Show your potential buyers how each room is used. Making the function of each room abundantly clear takes away the guesswork. Even if they may use the room differently, knowing that you have carefully planned the space will give them a sense of comfort and recognition that will work in your favour.

Space planning refers to the function of each room and traffic flow, as well as furniture layout.

Function. Clearly defining the purpose of each room makes it easy for your buyers to understand the layout of the house. Don't make them guess what the room is used for. When your buyers walk into a room, they should know exactly what it is used for.

Don't think that the buyer should be able to mentally clear out that gym equipment from your dining room because they won't, they'll get confused and you stand to lose a sale.

When you make it easy for your buyers to see how you live in your home, it will make it easier to visualize themselves living there and making it their home. Every room should be defined as to its intended purpose. Notice I said *intended* purpose.

One of the homes I was called in to stage had been on the market six months. The layout of the house was terribly confusing. There was an overhead chandelier in the living room, a treadmill and a set of weights! The buyers' were confused about the chandelier hanging low in a living room area. When they saw the gym equipment, they must have wondered why the house was so awkward that the living room had to be used for exercise equipment. When they tried to visualize living in this house, they were unsure about how their living room furniture would fit in and how the room would look if it weren't also a workout space. The potential buyers quickly lost interest and left to explore other homes.

When I came in to stage the home, we temporarily took it off the market. We relocated furniture from other rooms to furnish the living room with a sofa, armchair and coffee table. We then installed a new, updated ceiling light fixture and accessorized the room. It turned out that the basement was not only large enough for gym equipment, but it had a huge mirror installed on one wall. We moved the treadmill and television to the basement and set up the weights, making it into a functional gym. When we put the house back on the market, it sold inside two weeks.

In another one of the homes I staged, a bedroom was designated as a "dressing room" and used purely for hanging clothes on racks on either side of the room with an ironing board in the centre. This makeshift arrangement gave the impression that the home did not have enough closet space and a whole room had to be claimed to contain the clothes. First, we packed up all the out-of-season clothes and put them into storage. Then, we set up a double bed with side table and lamp with accessories in the room and put the remaining clothes into the closet. With this more comprehensible arrangement in place, the viewers could understand and appreciate the function of each room. The house sold in eight days.

Earlier I said that every room should be defined as to its intended purpose. A home office is a good example. This was probably not the intended purpose of the room when the home was built, but it's an increasingly common function for an extra room. The key is to make it a distinct home office. Do not distract viewers with other elements from a kid's playroom, a guest bedroom or a teenager's hangout, even if that's how it was actually used by your own family. Stick with all the Seven Steps in this system to make it into the best possible office there is. Your buyers will appreciate the clarity and, at the same time, fully understand that it can be turned back into a bedroom if they so choose. Technically, it is a bedroom as long as it has a clothes closet built in.

TIPS: Children's Toys. Children's toys can be notoriously distracting to a buyer. Inconvenient though it may be, children's toys should be located in a designated playroom – one that is not in a dark basement. The idea of sending your kids down to a dark basement to play is far too gloomy, and I've seen this many times in staging a home. Don't give your buyers a reason for negative emotions.

If you have no available space for a bright, cheerful dedicated play-room, then store toys into colourful rubber storage bins in the children's bedrooms during a showing. Get the kids involved in putting their toys away. Some of the toys – such as playhouses, pedal cars, toy kitchens, castles, etc. – won't go into boxes because they are so huge. These huge toys have to find a new home for the duration of the sale. They could be kept in a storage garage. Get the kids involved and help them understand that this is only a temporary loss until the house is sold, then they can have all their toys back. If the toys have outlived their popularity, then this is a good time to sell them or donate them.

If you have a nebulous space in your house, ask yourself these three questions: 1) What is the *intended* purpose of this area? 2) Who uses it? 3) When is it used?

Don't give your buyers reason to scratch their heads and wonder how places in the home are used. Make sure you are very clear about the use and purpose of every nook and closet. Extra rooms today are called Flex Rooms. Many viewers will be hoping to find such a room in your house. You do not have to set up the room to match their dreams of how they would use the room. Each viewer would use the space differently. The important thing is to give it a clear function, so they can transpose their own ideal function onto the room without confusion.

Whatever the other rooms are used for, make sure that there is at least one bedroom dedicated to being a bedroom exclusively and not shared with an office in the corner or any other disparate elements.

Corner nooks should not be left to fend for themselves. If you have a nook, placing a reading chair, a small table and a floor or table lamp turns it from a useless space to a cosy reading area.

Closets and cupboards should only contain those items meant for that space. That means that in the coat closet there must be no cleaning products brooms or vacuum cleaners. Check out your kitchen cupboards. Sort all the canned food together by categories: dry goods, pots and pans, dishes, glasses – you get the idea.

In the bedroom clothes closets, define the closet's owner and ensure that only those items that belong to that person are stored there. In bathrooms, store all regularly used personal items such as toothpaste, shampoo, and soap in a plastic basket and place it under the sink. Buyers will look under the sink, so make sure everything is in its place and is tidy.

Potential buyers are entitled to examine built-ins, such as bathrooms and kitchens to see that they work properly. If they are full of unrelated items, the buyer will assume that the house is too small for all your possessions, and if they believe it is too small for you, then they can more easily assume it will be too small for them.

Defining a purpose for each room, closet, cupboard and drawer will be particularly appreciated later on when you realize that you have made it super easy for a mover to pack your things and for you to locate and unpack your possessions in your new place! When all like-items are packed together, they arrive together. Many years ago I skipped this step and ended up finding the toilet plunger in with my crystal glasses. I didn't find my kettle until a year later, when it turned up with the camping equipment. I will never skip this step again.

Traffic Flow. You know you have a traffic flow problem when you bump your shin on the corner of the coffee table, or when you think the furniture is placed in the *only* possible configuration. If you have blocked off a rarely used doorway with a chest of drawers, or you or your pets can't move smoothly through the room because of obstacles in the way, then you need to rethink the placement of the furniture.

The idea is be able to arrive at your destination in a reasonably straight line without danger of tripping over or bumping into anything – that includes furniture, rugs, artwork, low hanging lamps, chairs, tables, and toys. The aim of planning your space is to create a fluid movement of traffic in and throughout the home, so you can move around comfortably. It is also another way of creating the illusion of openness and breathing space.

Furniture Layout. To save yourself the chore of lugging chairs and dressers around the room to find the best fit, do it first on paper.

1. Use a tape measure to find the dimensions of the room.
2. Draw the outline to scale on graph paper. (In a typical scale, 1/4 inch equals 1 foot.)

3. Make a note on your diagram of anything that will affect the arrangement of your room – electrical outlets, heat registers, windows, doors, light switches, etc.
4. Measure your furniture, make scaled cut-outs, and move them on the room diagram until a likely arrangement emerges.
5. Select a focal point for your room and adjust other furnishings and lighting toward it. Remember, a fireplace will nearly always be the focal point; other focal points might be bookcases or built-in shelving to house your collectibles, a sofa with striking artwork on the wall above it, or in a bedroom it would be the bed and headboard.
6. Arrange the furniture in such a way that pieces viewed as a unit don't show dramatic variance in height and mass as the eye sweeps the room. When a high-backed chair is next to a low table, for example, boost the visual height of the table with a table lamp or artwork positioned above the table.

In the living room, or large master bedroom, set up a cosy conversation area, this might include two love seats, facing each other. Alternatively, two chairs can be separated by a low coffee table.

Always pull furniture away from the wall to give the illusion of more space. This even works in a small room.

If you have a very large living room, use a sofa to divide the space. Put down an area rug so that it just catches under the front feet of the sofa to ground the space. Place a coffee table on the rug parallel to the sofa.

Furniture Arrangement Guidelines. In this section, you'll find the crash course on the rules of proportion and placement in staging your home. The main rules of thumb are based on human ergonomics. Following them not only results in harmonious spaces, but also helps avoid accidents.

- Group furniture to face the focal point.
- In an open concept space, group furniture into conversation areas. Place sofas and chairs facing one another for an intimate grouping or back-to-back to create two separate points of view.
- In a large, open space, anchor one or both ends of the room with substantial or tall items, such as an oversize painting, a mirror or a fireplace with art hung above it.

- Allow between 18" to 24" (45cm-60cm) for traffic flow through the room. Try to keep the flow as straight as possible from the door to the window
- Provide 16" to 18" (40cm-45cm) between the sofa and the coffee table to give you enough space to get around the table.
- Move furniture away from the wall 2"-3" (5cm-8cm) to give the illusion of more space.
- Place a rug in front of chairs/loveseat/sofa to ground the setting. Capture the legs of the furniture by 6"-12" (15cm-30cm) so that swinging feet do not kick and curl the edge of the rug.
- In the dining room, allow 36" (90cm) from the edge of the table to the wall for easy access in and out of the chair.
- Shift chairs and tables so you can move around comfortably.
- Arrange your bed in a conventional position. This is not the time to turn your bed diagonally within the room; this arrangement is inelegant to many people and might give the impression that there is no other place for the bed.
- Keep the bed headboard on longest wall if possible, so that you can walk around the bed easily. Putting the bed on the same wall as the door creates a traffic flow obstacle.
- Allow at least 24" (60cm) between the side of the bed and the wall.
- A dresser and the foot of the bed should be at least 42" (106cm) apart so you can open the drawers easily.
- Relocate any objects that obscure a door from opening fully.
- Use two-sided tape on rugs that can trip, or remove the rugs altogether.
- Take down artwork that protrudes into a traffic area.
- Lift low hanging lamps so they are no lower than 7' from the floor.
- Pick up toys that can trip and hide them in plastic bins.

Summary: *Make sure you are very clear about the use and purpose of every room. When buyers see the purpose of each room, it makes it easier for them to visualize themselves living there.*

Create a fluid movement of traffic in and around the home so you can move around comfortably – this is another way of creating the illusion of space.

STEP SEVEN – FINISHING TOUCHES

"Never be afraid to do something new.
Remember, amateurs built the ark;
professionals built the Titanic."

~ Anonymous

Tasteful accessories, striking vignettes and surprise memory hooks are another secret to making your home stand out from the rest. Many people stop before dealing with the most important part: accessorizing. Be aware that the best final additions mark the fine line between sterile and overstuffed. The home should preserve its lived-in-and-loved atmosphere while maintaining stylish and up-to-date good taste. This is the make or break part of all of the above.

Your furniture and accessories must complement rather than compete with the architecture. Dressers, bookshelves, and mantles all become more beautiful with a little attention. Accessorizing should reach each one of the five senses; remember, a home is purchased largely through emotions, and there is no better way than by awakening the five senses.

Wall Décor and Artwork. Adding these elements to your walls can create a warm, welcoming feeling. Do not feel you have to position something on every wall. Remember, less is more. It is okay to leave one or two bare walls in a room.

Don't despair if you don't have any artwork for your walls. For very little effort and little cost, purchase a few inexpensive unfinished wood frames from thrift stores, big box stores, flea markets or craft shops that you can paint. Then get creative. If you travel, gather five or six of your favourite travel photos and create a gallery wall. Print your photos in black and white or sepia tones to make the subject matter appear more important and artistic.

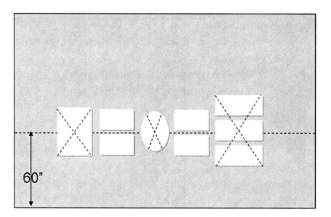

Picture placement on a gallery wall.

Quick, easy and low-cost, yet sophisticated prints and single-sheet gift wrap can be obtained from a quality stationery stores. They often look as though they were intended to be framed in the first place. Deeper, shadow box frames can be used to store and show off your most cherished childhood book or a collection of contemporary miniature books. Grouping miniature items together can provide interesting décor. Consider a certain theme for any grouping you plan on making for various areas of your home, and don't overlook your kid's artwork – matted and framed; it can often pass as a masterpiece!

If you still haven't found anything to frame, look outside to nature. Pick interesting leaves or grasses. Get down and dirty with creative stamps cut from potatoes. No frames? Then print off pictures to fit inside old empty CD cases, glue a ribbon to the back and hang four or five in a vertical row.

Controversial Artwork. Do not put yourself in the position of offending any of your viewers. There are many people who could be upset by art or accessories that they consider distasteful art. It's best to remove artwork or accessories that might in any way be construed as offensive.

Controversial items are nude photographs, taxidermy, items that involve aspects of religion or religious shrines, cremation urns, intimate personal items (yes, I have seem them all), including the whips and chains, which, trust me, are major distractions. You must ensure that your viewer will not be sidetracked.

Remove certificates, awards, diplomas and any other clues of who you are, what you do, or how successful you are. If the buyers perceive your position in life as being affluent, then perception is their reality; in some cases this could have a negative effect on the price of your home. If the belief is that you are wealthy, then you can afford to drop the price. Whether you are affluent or not you warrant the most from your investment.

Positioning Artwork. It is important that artwork is positioned at the correct height. Hung too high and the ceiling will appear low. If hung too low, the wall above the picture will appear lost and out of balance. The rule of thumb when preparing your home for sale is to make sure the centre of the picture is 60" (152cm) from the floor.

Whatever people say, size does matter. To be pleasing in proportion to the room, artwork placed above a chair, sofa, loveseat or chest should occupy approximately two-thirds to three quarters the width of the furniture. It should be positioned so that the bottom of the artwork is about 8"-10" (20cm-25cm) above the furniture, or two fists high.

Mirrors. Use mirrors in every room. You simply cannot have too many. Use them to make the area appear more spacious and brighter. Always check to be sure that their reflection is worth repeating. Do not hang a mirror that reflects an unappealing view (i.e. a bathroom, a factory or a blank wall).

To gauge how to position a mirror on the wall, use the same rule of thumb for artwork: the centre of the mirror should be 60" (152cm) from the floor. When placing a mirror above a chair, sofa, loveseat or chest of drawers position it 8"-10" (20cm-25cm) above the item. To balance the effect, size the mirrors to occupy approximately two-thirds to three quarters the width of the item below it.

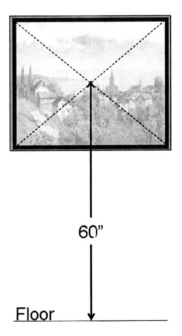

Artwork placement.

For a narrow space, hang several small mirrors in a horizontal row to help it to appear wider. If you want to visually increase the height of your ceilings, hang several small mirrors in a vertical row instead.

A mirror in the foyer will make this often small area appear larger and it is practical for checking appearance before going out. A full length mirror in the master bedroom is a must.

Positioning artwork over furniture.

Small or lightweight mirrors can be hung just like any other picture. But if you have invested in a large heavy mirror, you need to take extra care in hanging it. This is especially true when hanging on drywall. Unless you are lucky enough to have a stud right behind where you are planning to hang it, there are steps you need to reinforce your hooks so your mirror won't come crashing down!

If you have a corner of a room in your home that seems dark and unwelcoming, place a mirror there. The mirror will reflect the light from the room back out and help to brighten the corner. If the corner is really dark and you don't have a lot of light in the room to begin with, try purchasing a lighted mirror or a mirror with a small shelf on it where you can place candles or a small lamp. The mirror will double the light from the light on the shelf and really help brighten the corner.

For people who live in apartments or condominiums, window light can be limited. By adding a mirror or group of mirrors to those windowless walls, you can create the illusion of windows and reflect light into the space. Mirrors mounted inside old window frames with curtains hung either side of them can further enhance the illusion; this is especially effective in a basement.

Collections of mirrors can be used instead of traditional art behind a sofa or in a hallway. Start with a large mirror and hang smaller size mirrors around it for an informal, eclectic feel. For a home full of antiques, you can choose mirrors with similar antique style frames, such as gold leaf. Whitewashed frames will compliment the shabby chic look, and identical small framed mirrors hung in rows will contribute to the look of a modern interior. Instead of the traditional wall-to-wall mirrors used to make a room seem larger, the trend now is to use a row of long, tall mirrors spaced across the wall.

Walls are not the only place for mirrors. Long, narrow mirrors are perfect under the centerpieces on dining room tables, (especially delightful for romantic, candlelit dinners.) A cut-to-fit mirror can serve as the perfect cover for the top of a worn side table. Add a lamp or candles and you increase the sparkle in that corner of the room.

Mirrors can also be found in unexpected places, placed in the back of display shelves they help show off your collections and figurines. Even if placed in the back of pantry shelves mirrors can reflect light and help locate items on deep shelves. Let mirrors reflect your good taste (excuse the pun, I couldn't resist it).

Window Treatments. The purpose of window dressings is to show off a beautiful view, or cover an ugly view, or to provide privacy, or protect furnishings and floors from the harmful UV rays of the sun in a south-facing room. You could consider doing without a window dressing altogether if you have a beautiful view, no privacy issues and the room is not south-facing. It might be enough to simply paint the window frame the same colour as the trim (baseboards, doorframes, etc.). To give a softer look, install drapery or sheer panels either side of the window to frame the view. If the window is south-facing then it would be wise to consider panels and retractable UV rated pull down blinds, or panel track blinds to protect walls, floors and furnishings from fading. Your buyers will thank you for it and you will most certainly get a return on your investment.

For windows that require coverings for privacy, hang sheers and full panel, lined draperies that coordinate with the wall colour or furnishings. Play up a room's assets. If it has high ceilings, put up really tall curtains.

Whatever you do, please get rid of the lacy granny curtains. They are terribly dated, hideously ugly, collect the dust, and smell awful. (I hope that's a strong enough message for you.)

In one of my homes, I had to dress a bare window in a bedroom for privacy, so I went to a thrift store and found a set of sheers for $5 that just fit the window. They weren't in great condition, but with a little careful arranging, I could hide the flaws and they would do the job. When I fashioned some tie backs from some silk ivy leaves, they looked amazing.

My buyer loved them so much that she put it into the Condition of Sale that I leave those window sheers. Unfortunately I didn't pay attention to that detail and took them down. I really didn't think anyone would want $5 drapes at their window. Of course my buyers didn't know that they were thrift shop bargains. My naivety was exposed. I got a legal letter demanding that I replace them immediately.

The trouble was, I had already donated them back to the thrift store. I was sure I'd never see them again, but the patient store assistants and I dug them out. I paid another $5 for their trouble and my reputation was saved. The moral is: Don't underestimate the power of a set of thrift shop curtains – and pay attention to the Condition of Sale!

Furniture. We have talked about how to arrange your furniture. Now we need to talk about the furniture you arranged. I hear it all the time: "My furniture doesn't match," or "My furniture is old fashioned." The most common is, "My furniture is ratty." If you own a selection of mismatched furniture, relax, it will work providing it is in reasonable condition.

The secret is the pleasing colour coordination of your soft furnishings, couch, armchair, loveseat and draperies. As the Colour chapter explains, all your soft furnishings should fall within the colour categories of analogous or complementary to make the room appear interesting.

If your pieces don't coordinate with one another – or all fall in the category of ratty – one option is to use new large coordinating bed sheets to cover your sofa, chair, and loveseat. Pin and tuck the ends in and all around. However, sometimes that won't work because of the style of the furniture, so your second option is to consider using slipcovers. Don't be worried about soft furnishings not matching *exactly*. In fact, the matchy, matchy look can be boring and predictable. As long as the colours are in harmony and you have kept patterns to just one or two pieces, the look will succeed.

If none of the above works and you don't want to permanently give up your cherished mismatched, and old fashioned furniture, you might consider putting it all into storage and replacing it with rented furniture. You'd be surprised how much the expense is worth it. This option does pay off in the long run.

What do you do about continuity if you have a mixture of different woods in a table and sideboard? These days, trends dictate that it is more desirable to have different coloured wood pieces than having all woods the same.

If you have a room filled with beautiful antiques, give it a modern twist by adding one modern piece, a chair, a table, a lamp. Conversely, a room filled with modern, contemporary furniture will be more appealing with one fabulous antique. Both looks impart design drama.

For a bedroom, it is absolutely worth buying fresh new bedding. The bed-in-the-bag idea is perfect for staging your master bedroom through to your spare bedroom. A bed-in-a-bag includes a bed skirt, a cover and pillow shams and in some packages you also get a bottom and top sheet and pillow cases that all coordinate, taking out the guesswork.

Photographs. Displaying personal photographs are always a subject of hot debate when it comes to staging your home. The questions most asked are whether to leave them out or to put them away. We all display personal photographs to remind us of loved ones and of happy times. Personal photographs show that the home is occupied and loved by real people. Portraits of children, parents, or ancestors are all acceptable to place on view. The whole idea of staging your home is to help your viewers to absorb and emote with the architecture of the home.

Do not display photographs which are high spirited, cutesy or provocative, however. To be specific, avoid weddings, family outings, naked babies or boudoir portraits. You will be in danger of defocusing the attention of your viewers. To be on the safe side, pack away any you are not sure of and keep those you want to display in moderation. Displaying one, three or five in a collected area is tasteful.

Mantles, Shelves and Surfaces. Decorating a mantle for a staging is simple. These elements are: wall décor, accessories, greenery, and lighting. This technique is called The 3+1 Method.

1) Wall Décor. Select the wall décor you wish to display above the fireplace. It may be a painting, a framed photograph, a piece of decorative ironwork, a mirror, or a tapestry – whatever appeals to you. A mirror is popular over a fireplace, it makes your room appear larger and brighter, but always be sure it reflects something pleasing.

As a rule of thumb, you need to keep the artwork within two-thirds the size of the mantle. If it is any larger, it can overwhelm your fireplace! Some artwork can be propped directly on the mantle, but if you choose to hang your artwork, place it 4"-10" (10cm-25cm) above the mantle.

2) Accessories. Taking into account the colours in the artwork, select three accessories in cascading sizes to coordinate with the artwork. These will be grouped at one end of the mantle. Then select one accessory of similar visual weight for the other end.

3) Greenery. Bring in warmth and life with greenery. Tuck it around and through the single large accessory.

+1) Lighting. Add ambience with lighting. You could position a light over the artwork, on the floor or on a table close to the fireplace.

In the winter, finish off the look by placing rustic fire-irons on the hearth. Even if you have an electric or gas fireplace, it will give the illusion that the fire is real.

In the summer, replace the fire irons with a pot of flowers and greenery. If your firebox is wood burning, then empty out the ashes and replace with a pile of silver birch logs, pinecones and flickering LED candles.

Decorating a mantle or shelf using the 3+1 method.

On a bookshelf, books and other items should occupy just two-thirds of each shelf. Books can be stacked one on top of the other or left standing with a bookend on either side. Add one, three, or five interesting items to each shelf such as travel souvenirs, mismatched picture frames, or a collection of something you love. Leave empty spaces to show there is room to breathe and the effect will be more pleasing to the eye.

Simple is best. Surfaces such as a bedside table need only the bare necessities, such as a lamp and an alarm clock – nothing more.

On a shelf in the foyer or hallway, place just one small container for keys, etc.

On a dresser, select one or three items in cascading sizes, which means, one large, one medium and one small item grouped closely together. Get rid of any doilies.

Select opposite shapes for your surfaces. For example, put a square object or an angular dish on a round table to create contrast and interest. Put a round vase on a square table. On a side table, place three items closely together, such as a vase, a small clock and a framed picture of someone you love.

Toss Cushions and Cosy Throws give you the opportunity to add analogous colour for a soothing and calming effect or complementary colour for added pizzazz. Keep in mind the one, three, five rule and arrange the cushions on sofas, beds, and chairs. A coordinating throw finishes the look and gives added cosiness. Vary the textures to add interest and appeal.

Flooring. Rugs are wonderful accessories. They come in faux fur, silk, wool, synthetic and shag. Today's shag is beautiful – a huge leap from the '70's shag wall-to-wall which was hard to vacuum and needed raking to keep it attractive. *We've come a long way, baby!*

When it comes to flooring, most buyers favour the natural look of hardwood. You can bet that out of all the types of flooring, hardwood floors will have the most longevity and will not go out of style. If you cannot afford hardwood, a synthetic wood floor is always a good option. Avoid a laminate floor; it will not fool anyone - it has a hollow sound when you walk on it and it does not look authentic.

Ceramic floor tile is an elegant and stylish flooring material that comes in virtually any colour, texture. It is both tough and durable. It can be installed in most any room; however, it is most commonly used in kitchens and bathrooms. Its benefits are its versatility, variety, durability and its ease of maintenance.

Hardware and Fixtures. Replacing knobs and drawer pulls in kitchens and bathrooms is the quickest way to update a bathroom or kitchen. When it comes to faucets, you can buy something infinitely better than what you already have for very few dollars. Buyers invariably prefer the coordinated look that rises above standard builder's grade.

It is that subliminal thing again. We do not consciously inspect doorknobs, faucets and cabinet knobs, but when they are dated or mismatched, we get the feeling that the home is shabby.

Other Accessories. In home staging, we have to use accessories that will appeal to the largest audience of potential buyers. Your accessories tell your story; make it one worth knowing. Accessorizing with personal objects is the way to give a home your imprint. Indulge in the extraordinary.

Are you a collector? Remember in the Clutter section you were asked to hold back one, three or five items? This is where positioning accessories works every time: Display a pared-down collection of five or seven of your favourite pieces. Designate a bookcase or shelf to group your pared down assortment of collectibles.

Keep the accessories big and bold. Fiddly little accessories become visual noise, otherwise known as clutter. If your items are small, then group them together closely in groups of three or five pieces.

Fresh same-colour flowers and fresh candles give a lived in and loved look to which buyers gravitate.

When accessorizing, look to the dollar stores or big box stores for items that will enhance and renew without costing a fortune.

Sensory Cues.

Take care to appeal to all five senses. Try to make all your finishing touches reach each one of the five senses. Never forget: A home is purchased largely through feelings. There's no better way to evoke pleasing emotions than by awakening the five senses.

Lemons invigorate, Lavender and Cinnamon evoke memories of home.

Smell. Our sense of smell connects to our memories. The smell of popcorn can remind us of being at the movies with a friend or salt in the air can remind us of the beach.

Scents such as lemon suggest freshness. Vanilla, freshly baked bread, cinnamon, cloves, lavender and honey all evoke memories of home, relaxation and wellbeing. Using two or more of these gentle scents is another way to use layering. It is a great memory hook for your home.

On the opposite side of the scale, unpleasant smells, such as mould, stale cigarettes, damp rags, dust and wet dogs, put people off. Never use fragrance sprays to cover up smells. Your discerning buyers will be onto this immediately, and many people today with allergies are offended by heavy perfumes. Buyers can detect this cover-up in a heartbeat.

Above all, make sure your home smells fresh and inviting. The best start is to make sure it is sparkling clean; nothing can beat cleanliness.

Keep in mind that it is important to keep fragrances subtle in your home. The idea is to keep the scent almost indiscernible. In a bathroom, display new fragrant soaps and a beeswax candle. Set beeswax candles and a bowl of potpourri on surfaces in the living room, family room, and bedroom. An unlit beeswax candle emits a wonderful, but very subtle honey aroma and the potpourri adds a continuously fresh fragrance. Freshly baked bread and cookies are always welcome. One of my clients put a loaf of bread in the oven prior to each viewing – the same loaf. After the second baking it was inedible and as hard as a doorstop, but the fragrance remained.

>**TIPS: For Freshness.** Some other items for providing low-cost, unlimited freshness in your home:
>
>- Laundry dryer sheets can be used to freshen the air in almost any location from closets to wastebaskets, suitcases, fans and vacuum cleaners.
>- Baking soda or vinegar with lemon juice in small dishes absorbs odours around the house. Remove them before the showing.
>- A cut lemon can be rubbed around the insides of your kitchen sink and laundry tub.
>- Cinnamon and cloves can be simmered in water or apple juice on stove. Remove before a showing.
>- Bowls of fragrant dried herbs and fresh flowers can be placed in the room.

Sound. Our sense of hearing allows us to interact with and to be more aware of the environment around us. Sound in your home during a showing must be subtle. The volume of sound should be at around 30dB. Now I am showing off – no one I know has a decibel meter kicking around. But if I tell you that a whisper rates at 20dB, normal talking is between 50-60dB and an alarm clock registers in at 80dB, you will get the idea.

If your home is on a noisy street, keep the windows closed and focus your buyer's attention on the inside environment. Listening to relaxing sounds transforms silent homes into a soothing atmosphere. Some sound ideas for providing a memory hook in your home would be to play soft music in the background. A water fountain is renowned for its relaxing and healing powers and adds a visually stunning focal point guaranteed to please the ears, eyes and the soul.

Do any of your rooms resonate with an echo? If so, this could be due to lofty ceilings, hardwood floors, ceramic tiles, granite countertops, leather furniture, large windows, etc. When there are large areas of smooth surfaces, sounds tend to bounce around making for an unpleasant atmosphere. Deadening echoes is an easy task; in a living area, put in a large area rug, fabric window dressings, fabric throws and cushions, and in bathrooms, use towels fabric shower curtains, etc to help absorb the ricocheting sounds.

Sight. In the summer months make your home look magical with faux candlelight. Get creative by grouping faux votives on your front steps, next to your door and into potted plants for a little surprise twinkle of light. Suspend groups of hanging votives from bushes and tree limbs so they look like fireflies in the summer night. It's also fun to float tea lights in a birdbath. Because they are faux candles, you won't have to worry about them being extinguished by the wind and rain.

My favourite, beeswax candles, provide welcome stimuli for two senses: sight for their beautiful natural colour and smell for their gentle scent. That sweet, natural honey scent also inspires serenity and romance. When one of the candles is illuminated, it also invigorates; its ion producing benefits are known to be an aphrodisiac for the body and soul. Need I say more? Be sure to snuff out the wick before the showing!

Real flowers and greenery add life and colour to a room. If you do not have a green thumb, then purchase silk greenery, which today looks so real you have to touch it to know the difference. Discard any sun-faded or cheap faux greenery.

Add pizzazz or calm with toss cushions, cosy throws and accessories that pick up and radiate colour.

Taste. One of my clients liked to bake cookies and, because she was on a diet, she left them on a plate with a note for the viewers to please help themselves. And they did! These tasty cookies engaged two senses: taste and smell.

Touch. While your other four senses, sight, hearing, smell, and taste, are located in specific parts of the body, your sense of touch is found all over. The sense of touch in this context is most noticeably with varying textures.

Include interesting textures when you are selling your home which far outweighs a variety of patterns. Let your eyes start with the floor and travel upward. As your eye travels upwards from the floor, notice how you can incorporate different textures with floor, wall and furnishings' textures, such as a shag rug, silk bedcover, a leather loveseat, and a glass coffee table. If you use too much of one material, it won't feel balanced.

Consider accessorizing with materials in a simple mix of organic products: tall vases of twigs, soft, silky grasses, smooth pebbles, beautiful shells and interesting feathers displayed in decorative pottery. If you have a glass table, top it with a wood, metal or ceramic dish. A glass bowl on a glass table adds nothing and its effect is lost.

Memory Hooks. Buyers typically look at dozens of homes over the course of several days, and even with notes and photos, those tours can start to blur. Among all the other homes your viewer's will be visiting, your home must provide something they will remember. You want to leave an impression. What will they say about your home?

Displaying a specific, simple item in your house that will leave a positive impact is called a Memory Hook. It could include:

- A beautiful garden.
- Hardwood floors.
- Great lighting.
- High tech toys.
- Interesting, bold accessories.
- Books help warm up a space. Large coffee table books stacked high next to a reading chair looks casual and inviting.
- Candles look great in clear glass vases. Fill the vases with rocks for winter and sand in summer.

If the focal point in your room needs "punching up", then add a touch of red or yellow, as in red apples or lemons. As you'll remember from the Colour section of this book, red and yellow are advancing colours. A bouquet of yellow roses will have a much greater impact than a mixed bouquet. Also avoid a mixed bowl of fruit, which amazingly enough can leave a cluttered look. Put out a bowl of shiny red apples or a container of fresh lemons in the kitchen to give maximum impact. Next to the bowl of red apples, place two shiny red coffee mugs and a neat pile of red tea towels. The same with the lemons, with yellow accessories placed within close proximity. A vase of short-stemmed yellow roses placed on the dining room table, expresses a classy look.

The biggest secret of all is to make each room look its best; clean, tidy, and loved without looking staged. It doesn't matter about how much effort you put into staging, your buyer will only remember the general welcoming atmosphere of the house, and not the individual tricks you have used to seduce them.

Summary: The finishing touches are a fine line between sterile and over-stuffed. The home should preserve its lived-in-and-loved atmosphere while maintaining stylish and up-to-date good taste. All finishing touches should include wall décor, accessories, florals and greenery, fragrance in the form of soaps, potpourri or candles and touch on each of the five senses.

PART THREE

Chapter Six

Making It Work

"Once you make a decision,
the universe conspires to make it happen."

~ Ralph Waldo Emerson

Applying the Seven Steps to Home Staging. Pay attention to the six most important areas in the home: the Foyer/Entranceway, the Kitchen, the Dining Room, the Living/Family Room, the Master Bedroom and the Bathrooms. How can you make your home attract interest within days of putting it on the market? By using the Seven-Step System

1. ***Red Flags*** are the most important of all the elements. When selling your home, you must attend to problems *before* your buyer points them out. This shows that your home has been maintained and that it is loved. In the long run, it will earn you a considerable amount of money.

2. ***Clutter*** is visual noise. Watch for obvious clutter and hidden or subliminal clutter. Clutter can be a complete turn off and negatively impact the sale.

3. ***Focal Points*** direct the eye to an area. Upon entering a room, this point focuses your attention and grounds the room.

4. ***Colour*** is critical to making or breaking a sale. Colour can change the way a room "feels" without changing its dimensions. Colour also affects the emotions and has different meanings in different cultures.

5. ***Lighting*** is instrumental in setting the mood of any room. Using multiple types of lighting in a room will create very dramatic effects. Lighting can create the illusion of changing a room size, height and width.

6. ***Space Planning*** is about defining the purpose of the room and how to generate a fluid movement of traffic in and throughout to create the illusion of space.

7. *Finishing Touches* delineate the fine line between sterile and overstuffed. Your home should preserve its lived-in and loved atmosphere while maintaining stylish and up-to-date good taste. All finishing touches should reach each one of the five senses.

Now that you are familiar with each of the Seven Steps, let's walk through your house and apply them to your rooms. Your potential buyers start evaluating your home long before they come in the front door. Their assessment starts at the curb. So our home staging has to start at the curb, too.

Curb Appeal

Start your Seven Step System at the curb – hence 'curb appeal'. First impressions are often what makes or breaks a sale. Most buyers make up their minds within the first nano-seconds. If they don't like what they see, they won't even get out of the car.

The fact that they arrived at all shows that you have made your photographs inviting enough to have a viewer make an appointment to visit your home. But if they pull up outside and see that it is untidy and unkempt – maybe a momentary lapse in your efforts to keep the front yard in top shape – you have given them a reason to drive on by. An unkempt house is unappealing. Subconsciously, they are thinking that if the owners have not had the time to tidy the yard, it is unlikely they have taken the time to maintain the inside of the home.

Make sure you follow each of the Seven Steps. If one of those steps is missed, then you may have also missed a possible sale. In today's competitive market, an attractive curb appeal is vital to enticing your buyers through the door. If your home has curb appeal, the buyer's emotions will be stirred and they will enter your home in a positive frame of mind.

Survey the scene and follow the Seven Steps to putting your home in order.

Red Flags: Identify and start fixing things immediately. The first problem might be that your buyers can't find your house because the number is obscured. Make sure the number is not hard to read because of neglect or because it is blocked by branches. Fix uneven walkways, unpainted window frames, broken garage doors, broken outside lighting, cracked walls, damaged downspouts, loose gutters, a dilapidated roof, dirty windows, random cobwebs, and unpainted fences in poor condition. In the growing months, plant flowers or purchase potted plants from the supermarket or nursery and place them around and through the greenery in your front garden. Re-sod a shabby lawn. If your target market includes buyers with young children then don't even think about putting in a concrete patio or rock garden because those buyers will be drawn to spaces with a flat, open lawn. A flat yard is a real plus. Spend some money and put in the grass. It's a good seller.

Clutter: Clear up obvious and subliminal clutter, such as children's toys, dog's bones, broken furniture, dead plants, untidy log piles and any other debris. Clear clutter from both exterior and interior window sills, etc.

Focal Points: The front door is the most important feature of the house and should be attended to as the focal point. Show it up. This is where *Colour* and *Focal Points* blend. Neglect the front door and your potential buyers could neglect you.

Colour: Look at the neighbourhood homes and refresh the paint on your front door to make it stand out. Ideas for paint colour can be taken from the paint brochures found at do it yourself stores. Don't neglect to treat the trim to a fresh coat of paint. Here's a little tip, deep, dark red or jet black makes an eye-catching statement and adds panache.

When painting the front door, do not be tempted to paint the garage doors the same colour. The garage door should be low key and unobtrusive. Many garage doors are in the front jutting out from the house, and although an important asset, it is not the welcoming entry to the home, so keep the paint similar or the same colour as the house.

Lighting: Try to incorporate at least three of the five sources of lighting outside your house. At the very least, you will want: ambient lighting for overall illumination over the outside porch; task lighting such as solar path lighting to guide your visitors along a walkway; and accent lighting to highlight or spotlight objects such as a sculpture, trees, or walls. Automatic security lighting will increase the feeling of safety. Replace all light bulbs to highest allowable wattage. Clean all external light fixtures of cobwebs and dirt.

Space Planning: Check that your potential buyers can move from the curb to the front door on a fluid, unobstructed path. Check that steps, walkways and driveways are safe and easy to navigate. Trim overgrown trees; they must not block the view of the house, the house number or the light coming into the house. Ensure that it is perfectly clear where your property begins and the neighbour's ends. If the boundaries are ambiguous, consider investing in some fencing a brick wall or hedging plants. Make sure recycle bins and garbage bags are out of sight of front door (with the exception being garbage pick-up day).

Finishing Touches: Confirm that your doorbell works. Make sure the house number is displayed clearly and can be seen from the street. Place planters on either side of door. Get a new front door mat – preferably one that says *Welcome*. It gives an excellent subliminal message.

Polish the letterbox, door knocker and handle. Clean all windows inside and out till they sparkle. Go inside and arrange drapery or blinds so they are uniform, clean and presentable from the outside.

Curb Appeal.

Make sure your buyer sees and enters your house in a hopeful, optimistic frame of mind. The sad fact is that owners often don't see what a buyer will see and neglect this step. All the effort you make adds to the positive impact your buyers will carry with them when they enter the home.

The Foyer and Hallway

If your curb appeal was inviting enough to attract your buyers into the house, then congratulations, clearly you did a good job. Now, the buyers will have their first sight of the inside, as they enter your home. This is the first of the six most important areas in the home.

Stepping from the street into the foyer will create a lasting impression on your potential buyer. When viewers enter the home and are greeted with a bright, clean, fresh foyer, they are far more likely to continue their exploration and begin to imagine how *they* could live in this home; how *they* could take a shower in that bathroom; and how *they* could prepare a meal for their friends in this kitchen. That's where the emotional connection starts. A beautifully kept home, filled with love and attention no matter how big or small is more likely to lead to an interested buyer and successful sale. Continue with your good work and using the seven-step system pay attention to the foyer, the space that sets the mood for the rest of the house and see how easy it is to satisfy even your most critical buyer. Give the foyer and hallway the attention it deserves.

Red Flags: This is often the most used area in the entire house. Since it is the entrance and exit to your home, it takes a beating. Replace flooring if it is worn, replace the doormat. Check from floor to ceiling for flaws and problems. Look for damp spots and cracks in walls or ceiling. Is there a hall closet with a door off its track? Is the light fixture broken? Check that the newel post and stair spindles are secure. Is the floor worn, in need of replacing? Clean the interior door and doorknobs and give the walls a fresh coat of paint.

A Foyer Makeover.

When an open area has hardwood flooring and wooden or leather furnishing, such as in this foyer, there is often an echo which can be perceived as empty, cold and unfriendly. To remedy this, throw down an area rug and other soft furnishings such as armchairs and draperies to absorb the sounds and create a rich, warm welcome.

> *Who Knew? The Newel Post is main post at the foot of a staircase. In historic homes, the house plans were rolled up and placed inside the newel post once the house was completed and then the newel was capped. Could your house plans be in there?*

Clutter: The foyer and hallway is often a dumping ground for bags, coats and anything else. Fixing it up can require a lot of work. Look for items that don't belong in the closet, such as the vacuum cleaner, mop, and cleaning products. Remove out-of-season coats and give the closet breathing space. One third of the closet should be empty and nothing should be on the floor. Collect all those shoes kicking around on the floor in the foyer and put them on a shoe rack inside the closet. Hang up coats flung over the newel post.

Focal Points: Look for one primary element that focuses your attention. It could be a beautiful chandelier, an ornate coat tree, a stained glass window, a stunning mirror, or an antique grandfather clock. Make sure there is at least one item that stands out as the focal point.

Colour: In the foyer and hallway, follow the colour scheme for the rest of the house. The hallway should be a transition to other rooms. Artwork should follow the style of the home. A bright, fresh, welcoming entrance hall will create a lasting impression. Mirrors are both practical and give an illusion of space and no hallway should be without one.

Lighting: Bright lighting is essential in the foyer. Updating the light fixture is an easy and low-cost way to freshen the hallway. If you install a chandelier, make sure it is no lower than 7ft (2.2m) above the floor. When installing sconces along a staircase, pick a style that doesn't expose the light bulbs, so that they won't be visible to those ascending or descending the stairs.

If there is room, position an uplight under a floor plant or spotlight a large urn filled with dried and faux greenery to create interesting shadows and texture Always use light bulbs to the light fixtures' maximum allowable wattage. Clean light fixtures of cobwebs, bugs and grime.

Space Planning: So you don't have a foyer? Then make one. Many buyers don't like to just go through the front door straight into the living room. If you don't have a foyer, you have two choices. Outdoors, you can create an extension to your interior by building a vignette with a rustic chair, potted plant and a couple of lanterns, or a bistro table with two wrought iron chairs and urns with tall grasses. Indoors, this dilemma can be solved by using a console table, or a chest of drawers, or the back of a sofa to cleverly create an entryway. To keep the illusion of space, ensure that the artificial entryway measures no less that 36" (92cm) wide. Ensure there is a smooth path to adjoining rooms. Tuck chairs out of the traffic flow. See that artwork does not protrude. Remove rugs that can trip. Equip a small table or shelf for mail and keys. It is never a good idea to place keys on a hook by the door. I have friends who had their keys nicely placed on hand-made key hooks by the door made by one of their kids and labeled with the name of each car. They had a break-in shortly after and I'm sure the thief was super-grateful for the added convenience of knowing exactly which key belonged to the luxury car he drove away in.

Finishing Touches: Install a bold decorative mirror to check your appearance when you go out. Position a chair, if you have room, to sit on while taking off or putting on your shoes.

Remember to address the five senses. To satisfy the sense of smell, provide a natural scent at the front entryway with a beeswax candle or dip a cotton ball in a rich essential oil such as amber or teak and tuck it inside a vent. Fountain waterfalls add calm and serenity and increases peacefulness. The natural sounds of trickling water down a fountain waterfall can add a very organic and natural feeling to your home, instantly creating a soothing habitat to live in. Incorporate textures to satisfy the sense of touch: a shiny table, a big bold mirror, artwork, textured flooring, a crystal chandelier, an earthenware pot filled with greenery, an interesting umbrella holder.

The Kitchen

One of the six most important areas in the home, the kitchen is probably the biggest selling ticket you've got, so make the most of it.

The kitchen is considered the heart of the home. It is where everyone wants to gather when entertaining; where meals are prepared. You will want to show your buyers that the kitchen is bright, functional, welcoming and sparkling clean. Kitchen remodelling is typically the most lucrative form of home renovation when it comes to resale value. So updating and improving your kitchen is a wise choice – if you have the money to invest. Good remodelling ideas include replacing major appliances or countertops, adding custom lighting, repainting or replace flooring and building a kitchen island.

If you do consider a complete overhaul to attract your buyers, be careful to ask yourself in which price category is your house and how the changes you make will affect its resale value. A $200,000 house might only need minor upgrades to exceed the quality of all other homes in your neighbourhood, while a $400,000 house might need more extensive renovations in keeping with the neighbourhood competition.

It is imperative to take the housing market into consideration before you remodel no matter which price range your house falls into. Look into the current market and property values before beginning any project because the slower the housing market, the less money you will recover from your renovation, mostly because people will be paying less for houses.

Red Flags: Because the kitchen is such a central part of the home, it should be in top shape when buyers come knocking. The first task to ensure that your kitchen looks its best is to Red Flag it. That means looking at it with a critical eye to identify flaws, problems and glaring imperfections.

Attack Red Flags in the kitchen with a vengeance. Do not leave problems for the buyer to discover. It is far cheaper in the long run to fix it yourself or bring in the experts to take care of the problem than to negotiate with a buyer.

Fix dripping faucets or cracked tiles on the backsplash and floor. Clean the fridge and stove, inside and out, even if you are not intending to sell them with the house. Potential buyers may want to buy your appliances and can offer an attractive price for the convenience and aesthetics.

The sink will be scrutinized. Make sure it is clean and free of grime and grease. Use an old toothbrush to clean around faucets and use a dry cloth to shine and polish sink and surrounding areas. If it is badly scratched or chipped, the old sink is worth replacing. It is said that when your kitchen sink is clean, you will be compelled to clean everything else in your kitchen. Try it. It's amazing, it really does work.

Repair or replace linoleum or wood flooring that is stained, worn or damaged. While both of these projects are time consuming they can be done quite inexpensively if you are willing to put in some elbow grease.

It is also essential the cupboards look neat and clean, free of imperfections and stains, particularly since they take up so much of the kitchen space.

Provide proper ventilation. Install a fan above any cooking surface to allow the air to clear.

Think safety. When it comes to electrical outlets Ground Fault Circuit Interrupters, commonly known as GFCIs, are required for electric outlets in areas where water is used, such as kitchens and bathrooms. Should moisture enter the circuit or appliance, the electric power will be cut.

Have a fire extinguisher at hand. Position a home fire extinguisher in clear view, but not close to a cooking surface.

Clutter: Your next task is to identify and remove clutter. Remove all magnets from the fridge except for the one your real estate sales representative gives you. Take off pots and bric-a-brac from the tops of cabinets to make the ceiling appear higher. It's very easy to go overboard when decluttering the kitchen for resale viewing. I have seen surfaces completely cleared except for the adornment of a vase of flowers. No self-respecting chef would have a vase of flowers on their countertop, to do this screams "Staged!" Others have been so completely decluttered that it looks sterile; you could almost imagine performing surgery on the kitchen table. Make your kitchen *real* by displaying the most-used small appliances, such as a sparkling clean coffee pot, a brightly coloured juicer, a fresh set of coffee cups and modern, matching canisters. To do this, empty surfaces completely, then introduce select pieces to give the kitchen the lived in and loved look.

Focal Point: A kitchen's focal point might be fabulous granite countertops, an island with attractive barstools on one side, a stainless steel pot rack suspended overhead or a sparkling, stainless steel sink with a modern, prominent faucet.

The focal point will help determine the style of materials that will be used throughout the kitchen. If you've chosen an island as your kitchen's focal point, for example, and the island has a gleaming stainless-steel faucet, you'll want to make certain that shiny, silver-coloured elements appear here and there throughout the kitchen—perhaps as cabinet handles, drawer pulls and appliances.

When designing around a focal point, contrast and variety are just as important as repetition. The focal point should visually anchor the room. If your island surface and other countertops are made of high-gloss granite, choose a matte finish for the floor and backsplash tiles. Solid wood cabinets, as opposed to sleek laminate ones, contrast nicely with granite and soften its cold, hard appearance.

Colour: The kitchen is the heart of the home, where family and friends gather to enjoy each other's company. Creating a space with colour which supports this shared spirit can be a simple project. If you choose the right colour to paint your kitchen, you can create the most enticing room in your home.

Use the 3-step colour process to select your colour. Choose a colour that can be found in your counter top or cupboard doors when you shop for paint. For a staging, use three shades of a single colour to create a monochromatic colour scheme for your kitchen. This is particularly successful when neutral colours are chosen for a contemporary look or stay on the cool side of things by painting your kitchen a soothing shade of blue or green. These colours create a restful environment for the eyes and are well-suited to kitchens with a western exposure.

Choose paint in a medium colour of your chosen hue for the walls to help anchor the room. This shade should be lighter than the colour of your floors.

To give your kitchen an expansive feel, select lighter values for the ceiling paint. If you have a coffered ceiling, you can choose two colour values to make a contrast between the angled portions of the ceiling and the centre.

It is well worth updating any dark brown wood or painted wooden cupboard doors – that were in fashion in the 1970's – and replace them with new light pine or white doors. It will instantly brighten up the kitchen and make it look brand new. If that is beyond your budget, you are always safe to paint old kitchen cupboards white, which will also brighten the kitchen and make it appear larger, then add colour with accessories.

Lighting: Good kitchen lighting, from an aesthetic and functional standpoint, incorporates four of the five lighting techniques: ambient, task, accent and natural lighting. This method of layering the light is important for achieving positive results in all types of living and working spaces, particularly the kitchen. Think first about ambient lighting. This is the general, overall light that fills in shadows, reduces contrast, and lights vertical surfaces to give the space a brighter feel.

Many kitchens built in the 1970's have a California ceiling. This is basically a ceiling box with fluorescent tubes and is well suited to the job of providing ambient light. However this style of ceiling lighting is very dated. Its very design gives the illusion of a low ceiling. Replace this ceiling with recessed lights placed 3ft-5ft (1m-1.5m) apart on centre and 18" (46cm) from cabinets to light the countertops. (Note: Running the lights between two joists is easier than running through the joists.)

In addition, if you have at least 12" (30cm) of space from the top of the upper cabinets to the ceiling, place fluorescent tubes on top of the upper cabinets to indirectly reflect light off a light coloured ceiling, this is an inexpensive way to brighten up a kitchen. Fluorescent tubes have a bad reputation for casting an unattractive light, so choose 3000K or 3500K for a warmer, more inviting appearance.

The types and configuration of lighting in a room should be dictated, at least in part, by the focal point. You'll want lighting that not only accentuates the focal point's attraction but also maximizes its utility. Your task areas are best lit with bright, shadowless light. Pendant light fixtures look fabulous over a kitchen island; however, if you use the island as a busy workspace, a recessed downlight with a fluorescent bulb might be more appropriate. Install task lights on the underside of the upper cabinets, over sinks and tables.

Accent lighting is what gives our space a third dimension, adding to the quality of the space. Use this source of lighting sparingly on those special pieces that we want people to notice and admire, such as artwork, architectural details, collectibles, or a food presentation area.

Use dimmer switches on ceiling and under-counter lighting, if you can. Keep in mind, it doesn't work on fluorescent lighting. Every work space can use a bit of atmosphere. If you dim the lights in the evening when you aren't working in the kitchen, you will save electricity, too!

Ultimately, allow the light to flood in through windows. Remove fussy café curtains and replace with blinds, and remember, if you don't have a privacy issue, then dispense with window dressings altogether.

Kitchen Makeover.

Space Planning: This is the time to think about the space and flow in your kitchen. Use the 36" (92cm) rule-of-thumb. Ensure there is at least 36" (92cm) for walking between fixtures, appliances, and cabinets. If your floor plan has counter tops or cupboards with sharp corners that stick out, cut the corners or round them.

If possible, provide room for comfortable in-kitchen dining but avoid a cramped feeling. Keep your table small enough to allow a minimum of 36" (92cm) between the edge of the table and the wall. You'll have plenty of room to push back the chairs comfortably. You'll need a minimum of 36" (92cm) of counter top space for food preparation. Even if you take food from the freezer to the oven or microwave, you'll need some place to put the containers and serving dishes, so 36" (92cm) is a minimum. More is better. Washing and rinsing is easier if the sink is 36" (92cm) or less from the dishwasher.

Defining the space is particularly important for cupboards in the kitchen. Open a cupboard and decide what it should contain, rather than starting with what it does contain. Define and separate which cupboard will keep all canned food, all dry packaged food, plates, bowls, cups, mugs and drinking glasses.

So that you don't completely lose your mind while negotiating your newly organized kitchen, temporarily use sticky-notes on the cupboard doors for a few days to remind you and the rest of the family where everything goes. Be sure to remove the notes before the showing.

Make certain that the cupboards are only to a maximum of two-thirds full. Pack away extra dishes that aren't necessary. Show your buyers how spacious the cupboards are. Viewers have a hard time imagining they can get all their stuff in the cupboards when the cupboards are packed full with your stuff. You can be sure that during a showing cupboard doors will be opened and refrigerator interiors will be inspected. Any privacy will be a thing of wishful thinking.

Empty waste containers before a showing and then tuck them out of sight.

By following these rules you will assure a workable, safe, and convenient kitchen that will appeal to your prospective buyers.

The Finishing Touches: New handles and knobs can make a huge difference. Select hardware that complements the style and colour of your kitchen to draw these elements together. Don't be tempted to add kitschy little handles in the shape of a fork or vegetable. They can look tacky. Stay with sleek, up-to-date hardware. Consider brushed nickel or chrome hardware, if it ties in with your kitchen faucet.

A mirrored backsplash can help your kitchen to look larger and to feel more spacious. The light from the kitchen will reflect off the mirrors and down onto your countertops, providing additional light for cooking. The only stipulation is that the mirror must be impeccably clean. Splotches of water spots or dust will show up much more quickly on a mirror. The look is worth it, but you should know it will be higher maintenance.

Never be tempted to clear everything off your countertops to create the illusion of space. It doesn't work. It will have the same effect as an empty room. Without any comparison for size and function, the viewer will have a hard time envisioning how their toaster oven will fit on the surface and how all their stuff will look.

Make your kitchen real. Do not be afraid to display your beautiful shiny coffee maker or toaster. It's even better if they are coloured red or yellow and can be teamed with a bowl of bright red tomatoes or apples and a neatly folded red tea-towel. Get creative. Try yellow tea towels next to a colander of lemons or a basket of fresh carrots with green fronds attached and teamed with orange accessories.

Find an interesting pot and fill it with cooking utensils. You have no utensils fit to show in public? Then head down to the dollar store or big box store and pick up a set of matching utensils that you can plop into the container. Display interesting containers for coffee, tea, sugar, spaghetti. Accessorizing your kitchen does not have to cost and arm and a leg. Just keep it simple.

The Dining Room

One of the six most important areas in the home, the Dining Room is appreciated by buyers. Whether this room is formal or informal, whether it is a separate room or a part of other areas, such as the kitchen or living/family room, your dining room should always be planned around a table and chairs. Above all else, your dining room should be comfortable and inviting.

Usually, formal dining areas are in a separate room, while informal dining areas are out in the open, most often attached to the living room, family room, or kitchen. Be honest with yourself, while an elegant dining room with all the accoutrements may match your ideal vision of your life, most people who have formal dining rooms use them only occasionally. This is something to keep in mind when staging your home. A dining room that is used on a daily basis will be decorated more informally than a dining room intended for use only on special occasions. The important thing is to choose a formal or informal style and stick with it.

Red Flags: If the carpet is in bad shape, consider installing a hardwood floor. Today, there are so many varieties to choose from and many have been designed to make installation easy. Ensure that all wallpaper and decorative borders are removed.

Clutter: Once again, remember that less is always more in a small space. When you plan to add guests to the mix, the dining room can quickly look and feel too tight for comfort. Potential buyers who love to entertain will be aware of this. The greater sensation of space you can create in this room, the better. Remove all but dining-room related items from the room.

Focal Points: The focal point in a dining room is usually the dining room table and chairs. A buffet with a framed mirror above it, a chandelier, a painting, a grouping of photographs, a wall of French doors, or a large picture window can also dominate the room. Hanging an elegant lighting fixture, such as a crystal chandelier, always creates a fabulous focal point to the room. Whatever you choose as your focal point beyond your dining room table, you can place two dining chairs on either side to emphasize it and make it appear more important.

Colour: Because casual dining areas are so often open to other rooms, neutral colours tend to be the best choice for these spaces. Neutrals blend well with other colours, helping to create a complete, unified look.

Painting the wall a warm muted neutral – such as golden or creamy yellows, spiced oranges and terra cottas, wines, burgundies, and dusty roses – work especially well in more formal spaces. Psychologically, these colours help to stimulate the appetite, making them an excellent choice for rooms where the primary purpose is food and entertaining.

If you dare to consider brighter versions of these warm hues, especially vibrant yellows and oranges, be aware that these colours have a tendency to make people eat faster. That's why you see these colours in fast-food restaurants! If you use cool neutrals in this room, use warm colours as accents in your dining room, such as touches of red, orange or yellow, to stimulate the appetite.

Lighting: Try to incorporate all five lighting sources in your dining room. Using a combination – such as pot lights, lamps and a chandelier – is vital to the room because it creates layered lighting which adds depth and interest.

Getting the chandelier placement right can make all the difference to the ambiance of your dining room. Hang a chandelier so that the bottom is centered 30"-34" (76-91cm) above the top of the table. Choose one with a diameter that is at least *half* the width of the table.

Dining Room.

A buffet or sideboard can be flanked with wall sconces or buffet lights on either side. Choose fixtures that complement the style of your chandelier. Displayed objects can be accented with recessed downlights installed in the ceiling above.

Turn your china cabinet, hutch, or wall niche into a showplace for your prized collectibles by installing strips of low-voltage, mini-cone lights under the shelves.

It is also a good idea to have a dimmer switch installed in the dining room. This creates mood lighting, so that the dining room can become more versatile – easily making a transition from a romantic dinner to a child's birthday party.

Space Planning: If your dining room is small, keep your table sized to your room. Allow adequate room to move easily around the entire table, if necessary remove an extension leaf in the table. Place enough chairs around the table so that it looks comfortable and not crowded. Move extra chairs out of the room and into storage.

A dining room area rug should be at least 24" (61cm) larger than the table on all sides, so that the chairs can be moved in and out without getting caught on the edge of the rug.

Finishing Touches: Keep the décor in this room very simple. As I have said before, you simply cannot have too many mirrors in your home. Add a large mirror to one side of the room. This gives the illusion of greater depth, while also adding a fabulous element of decor.

Add life and energy to the room by placing a tall floor plant in a corner.

It is not necessary to dress your table as though you were serving a fancy dinner. Do not use a tablecloth – unless the tabletop is in rough shape and then only use a new colour-coordinated cloth that blends in with the room. If the table is in good condition, polish the surface instead.

Use a centerpiece on your table as the only decoration. Table centerpieces should match the season. If it is near a holiday, it is best for table center-pieces to match the theme of the upcoming holiday. The centerpiece should be less than 12" (30cm) high, so it doesn't overpower the table. You should leave a minimum of 4"-6" (10cm-15cm) of table space around the display. To create a very versatile centerpiece, lay a wreath of twigs on the table and fill the centre hole with a bowl of fresh seasonal flowers and greenery. Alternatively, you might also place a candle in the centre of the wreath and surround it with pinecones, or fill the middle with mini gourds and tiny pumpkins and surround them with fall leaves. Another option is to use an interesting pottery bowl that coordinates with the wall colour and fill it fresh lemons. For a high-impact contemporary look at a low cost, arrange three or five small bud vases in a line and fill each with a single flower of the same colour. Whatever you do, do not leave the table bare. Your centerpiece need not be expensive, just eye catching. Put your imagination to work!

Display single flowers for high-impact, low cost.

Make sure that all accessories in the room are proportionate to the main focal point. As a final touch, spray your chairs with fabric freshener for a clean, breezy fragrance.

The Living/Family Room

It may be called a living room or a family room. Where the living room and family room merge as one, it is called a Great Room. Whatever you call it, it can often show signs of too much life. This is the space where your family spends most of their time. Everyone watches television, listens to music, and entertains here. This room is one of the six most important areas in the home. It must be furnished to give your viewers a sense of how their furniture will fit into the space. It should make a statement. Make it easy for your buyers to appreciate the room's potential and architecture. If this room is warm and inviting, it will be a big drawing card to the sale of your home.

Red Flags: Fix typical problems found in the living room and family room, such as settling cracks in walls, damp spots, dirt and dust, worn or dirty flooring, wallpaper borders and dirty paint work. Address each of these problems and any others right away.

Living Room Makeover.

Clutter: Make a good start by clearing everything off window sills. Replace them with just one, three or five items grouped together, providing they will not interfere with light coming into the room. Remove family photos, trophies and framed certificates. Recycle magazines and newspapers that have accumulated. Pick up and put away toys and games.

Focal Points: A natural focal point in the living room is the fireplace. Emphasize its role by selecting a subtly contrasting colour for the walls.

If the mantle is unattractive, minimize its impact by choosing a wall colour that blends very closely with the mantle. If the room has both a fireplace and a television you have a dilemma. Since a fireplace is usually the item that is a fixture, group furniture to face and accessorize the fireplace you will either have to move the television another part of the house or move it out of the house completely – just for the duration of the move. In the picture above, we moved the television and heavy furniture to a basement room that we re-defined as the television room. We painted the fireplace white and the wall behind it in a dark colour and the surrounding walls a lighter shade in the same family. This really highlighted the fireplace. The new Berber carpet was our inspiration for the colour. The light, airy furniture was a great find from a local thrift store.

Some fireplaces are electric and can be moved. A fixed fireplace is an architectural feature that should be emphasized. If you have no fireplace, then use your television as the focal point and arrange all the main seating elements around it.

If your living room doesn't have a natural focal point, such as a cosy fireplace or a picture window with a scenic view, create one with an exceptional piece of furniture or a large coffee table arranged with interesting objects. Wherever the focal point is, surround it closely with seating to create a cosy conversation area.

If you do have a beautiful view, use it to your advantage. Frame the window with curtains and allow the buyer to enjoy the view.

Colour: Give the room a fresh new coat of paint in a light neutral colour to coordinate with existing furniture, as described in the Colour chapter. Bring colour and life into the room by using cushions, rugs, pictures and flowers.

Lighting: It is especially important to incorporate all five lighting sources in the room where members of the family and friends spend the most time. Start by checking to be sure there is sufficient ceiling lighting (ambient) in the form of a ceiling mounted lamps, or a fan with lighting incorporated, or pot lights. Then make sure you have sufficient floor and table lamps. When it comes to a living room, tradition has always held that it is best to have two matching table lamps for task lighting beside your sofa. This is not a strict decorating rule; in fact, it is trendier not to be all matchy, matchy. The secret is to ensure that the lamps convey the same visual weight and light intensity. To do this, make sure that the top of the table lamps are of equal height from the floor. The bottom of your lampshade should be at eye level when you are seated and the light bulbs should be of the same size, shape and wattage.

Next, check your spotlights for accent lighting to highlight a feature of the room. As mentioned, another accent light is the uplight; a very low cost, effective light source that looks terrific under a leafy plant.

Wall mounted lighting fixtures can be very effective. Their positioning can vary depending on the room, its furnishings and window placement. Mount sconces 10" (25cm) from the sides of artwork, so you do not crowd the art. Measure their centers to about 60" (150cm) from the floor to apply the rule-of-thumb horizon line as with artwork.

For natural light, open the curtains to let in the light. If the view would be better hidden, then hang sheers from the top of the window to the floor, so you can let in the light without subjecting yourself to the view. Multiply the width of the window by two or three to get the width of the sheer. It looks more luxurious to have a full sheer than one that barely pulls across the window. Your choice of living room curtains will be heavily influenced on how you use your living room. If it is a room that is in constant use, you will want to allow as much light in during the day and in the evening let your curtains provide privacy and impact.

If your living room contains some of your most prized furniture – family heirlooms, antiques, expensive couches and sofas, valuable framed pictures, or collections of china – then your living room curtains should be luxurious and formal. Use UV rated blinds together with expensive-looking fabrics like real or faux silks or damasks, with trimmings to match, so that you can protect your furniture and allow in the light.

If your living room is an informal room where the family hangs out to watch television or for casual entertaining, use less formal draperies, such as matchstick blinds or tab curtains.

Finally, position one or two new candles in the room on the coffee table or mantle. Don't overdue it with candles, too many can look tacky. Display them sparingly.

Space Planning: Arrange the furniture so that nothing obstructs an easy passage through the room. Remove any items that do not belong in a living room. Do not push furniture against the walls, but bring it slightly into the room to give the illusion of a larger space. To maintain the illusion of space, the height and depth of either side tables should match the height and depth of the sofa's arms as closely as possible. A coffee table should be about the same height or 1"-2" (2cm-5cm) lower than the seat height of the sofa. The length of a coffee table should be about two-thirds the length of the sofa (not including the arms). The width should be determined by how much room you have between the soft upholstered pieces and the table in your seating arrangement. Leave at least 16" (40cm) around each side of the table.

To ground your space, the living room area rug should be large enough that the front legs of all the furniture in a conversation grouping are on the rug. Never completely fill the room with the rug, there should always be at least 18" (46cm) of flooring between the rug edge and the wall.

Finishing Touches: Use subtle finishing touches to make the room look lived in and loved. Use coordinating toss cushions, a cosy throw, for comfort, texture, aesthetics and for colour. Place fresh potpourri or candles on surfaces. Group books on bookshelves according to size to create a feeling of uniformity. To generate a sense of space, leave room for one or two curios.

Artwork behind a sofa should take up wall space equal to one-half to two-thirds the sofa's total length. The width of a grouping of works includes the measurements of each piece, plus that of the spaces between them. Hang a grouping of pieces with equal space between each frame, 2"-3" (5cm-7cm) is best. Ensure that the bottoms of the frames are between 8" to 10" (20cm-25cm) from the top of the sofa.

The Master Bedroom

One of the six most important areas in the home, the master bedroom says more about you than you may like to admit. To get the most out of your bedroom, be sure it says what you want it to say. Let it be one of the rooms that makes an impact. It is important to give your viewers a sense of how their own furniture will fit into the space.

Red Flags: Remove any wiring that travels under the carpet. I have seen this done in a few homes. The problems stems from there not being enough power outlets. An electrical cable hidden this way in traffic areas is extremely dangerous.

Look for other problems in the room such as mold on the window ledges, squeaking doors and hard to slide closet panels. Closets that are more than two-thirds full indicate there is not enough closet space.

Check to see that rugs are secure. If the rugs curl, then roll them up, put them into storage, and show the beautiful hardwood underneath. If your floor is carpeting, then make sure it is clean and vacuumed before each showing.

Clutter: Yesterday's underwear and socks on the floor are perfect examples of what to avoid! Pick up clothes and shoes. Put them away in their designated place: the closet or the laundry hamper. Purge clothes in the closet until it is less than two-thirds full. This will give your viewers the chance to imagine their clothes in the closet. A little trick to make the closet appear even roomier is to pick up anything that is on the floor: shoes, boxes, etc., and put them up on shelves or on a shoe rack. Clear off shelves and surfaces completely, and then put back only one, three or five items grouped together. Take it one step further and replace your old coat hangers with fresh new, matching ones. It gives a sleek, clean, unified look.

Bedroom Makeover.

Focal Points: As you may have guessed, the focal point in your bedroom is Your Bed! Make this as fresh and comfortable looking as possible. Covers should be clean and smoothed out. The pillows should be plumped.

Colour The colour in your bedroom can be different from the rest of the home. Select your colour from the bed cover. Keep the colour a light muted neutral.

Lighting: It is a good idea to cover all five lighting sources into every room and this room is no exception.

Choose translucent lampshades so that the light comes through the shade, as well as above and below it, for a soft, romantic mood. You can add a chandelier if your ceilings are 9' tall or higher. It will add a very romantic air to the room. Install a ceiling light to an 8' ceiling. Position an uplight under a leafy floor plant in a dark corner to add interest and life.

Choose a bedside lamp that is tall enough so that the bottom of the shade is the same height as your shoulder when you are sitting up in bed.

Dress windows with privacy blinds overlaid with simple sheers, which are in demand now as part of the 21st-century urge to pare down. They diffuse the light and help make the room light and breezy.

Position an unlit beeswax candle to add a natural element. Open the blinds and draperies to let in the natural light.

Space Planning: Arrange the furniture so that you can walk directly from the door to the window without obstacles.

Your headboard should be on a wall and not under a window. This often means that the bed must be placed opposite the door. This is an excellent arrangement, since the bed is your focal point. It makes the bed the first thing you see when you walk into the bedroom.

Centre the bed on the longest wall, flanked by two side tables. Resist the temptation to place the bed under a window or at a jaunty angle in a corner. Never push it against the wall, this will cause the room to looked stuffed – and make one side of the bed inaccessible. For home staging, angled arrangements and squeezed-in furniture won't be appreciated or understood by your viewers. Always provide access to the bed from both sides. According to Feng Shui experts, a bed with access from only one side limits the open flow of communication between the partners. Besides that, it gives the illusion of the bedroom being cramped and the bed inconvenient.

Ideally, the height of the bedside tables should be within a couple of inches (5cm) of the height of the mattress, which can vary widely depending on the bed frame and the mattress design. Choose tables that have a large enough surface to accommodate a lamp, a clock, and a few personal effects, such as a book and reading glasses. Place the tables a few inches from the sides of the bed, so that reaching for items on the table is easy, but there is still sufficient space for bed making. Leaving spaces between the bed and side table also helps create an illusion of space.

Finishing Touches: Since this is one of the most important rooms in your home, spend some time to make it really inviting. Make sure the bedding is fresh. If your bedding is flat and uninteresting, then purchase a low cost bed-in-a-bag. This consists of a bed-skirt, a comforter, pillow shams and sometimes decorative pillows. Their low cost, high impact is well worth the effort.

On a dresser and chest of drawers, place one or three items only. Tuck jewellry and valuables out of sight. Get rid of fussy doilies and take the television set out of the bedroom altogether. Remember this inconvenience will only last for the duration of the sale. These efforts are designed to creating a stage that will attract buyers.

A full-length mirror in a bedroom is a must. It reflects light and makes the bedroom appear larger. Make the mirror bold and ensure its reflection is one worth sharing.

Accessorize each bedside table with a lamp. Place an alarm clock on one of the tables and a book on the other. No more that that! Don't be persuaded to add a tray with coffee mugs and a bud vase on the bed like the photographs you see in magazines. This effect looks contrived and makes it screamingly obvious the home has been staged.

Dispense with the frills and stuffed-animal shrines. Make your bedroom an inviting place to snuggle into. Using lots of cushions on the bed gives a warm welcoming feel. Be warned, however. I have seen a grown man scream when he saw how we had fashioned his bed to make it a focal point in the room. He is still grumbling to this day about how he had to fling off "a million" pillows before he could get into bed at night. His discomfort only lasted a short while, though, since his agent hammered the SOLD sign into his lawn three weeks later.

This is how you arrange cushions on the bed to give a designer look; first, two large coloured cushions go at the back, leaning against the headboard. In front, place two standard pillows in cases that match the sheets. Then for extra pizzazz, place two more standard cushions with decorative shams, matching the bedcover. Then, finish off the bed with one small cushion in a contrasting colour. That makes seven pillows – a lot, but not a million.

Decorative standard pillows are very low cost and fully worth the effort to make your bed look super comfortable and inviting. Another reason to consider getting new pillows is this, if your pillows are more than two years old, about 10% of their weight could be dust mite poo, dead mite bodies, human skin flakes and the skeletal remains of other bugs. . .sleep tight!

The Bathroom

The bathroom falls into the category of one of the six most important areas in the home. Like the kitchen and bedroom, your bathroom is one of the most frequented spaces in your home. It absolutely must leave your buyers confident that it is functional and clean! Why not take the time to make it just a little less ordinary ... and a lot more luxurious?

Fortunately, updating your bathroom should be as sound an investment for your home as updating the kitchen. These are definitely the two hottest investment areas for your home improvement.

A bathroom is also one of the hardest-working spaces in the home. If it's not functional, everybody is affected. Keep its purpose in mind. Consider it a workstation for preparing for the day ahead and a sanctuary for resting and recovering at the end of a hectic day.

Giving your bathroom a few personal touches is a must. But be aware that it is easier to over-invest in your bathroom upgrades than in any other room in your house. If you over-invest, you could be pricing your home above the market value for your area. Look around you and find out the prices of the classiest homes for sale that are similar to your own. Find the ceiling price for your type of home and budget all your remodelling costs to fit well into that price. It is so important to work out your budget before you begin to look and buy. Your bathroom-remodelling budget will help you to choose wisely and realize a wonderful new bathroom that will suit your home and your pocket.

Bathroom Makeover.

Red Flags: Obvious red flags to look out for are leaking pipes, trickling toilets, dripping taps, calcium deposits, mould and rust stains. Look also for damp spots under the sink. Get to the root cause and fix the problems. Dig out and replace old blackened grouting. Fill in missing grout from tiles. Consider installing a new 6-litre toilet if you currently have a water guzzler. Scrub sinks, tubs and toilets. Clean every surface until it sparkles. That includes areas *around* the sink and toilet. Remove mildew from showers and bathtubs.

Look for subliminal red flags. Yellowed toilet brushes are a real turnoff. Replace them with new ones. Remove the toilet plunger that has become a fixture for the past few years, even though you only used it the once. Astute buyers will wonder why a plunger has earned a permanent residence in the bathroom. Check that towel rails and toilet roll holders are secure. My favourite pet peeve in the bathroom is carpet. It doesn't belong in a bathroom, where it can become an open invitation to mildew and bacteria. Rip it out and replace with vinyl or tiles.

Clutter: Start by bringing two boxes and a garbage bag into your bathroom. Label one box "Necessities" and the other box "Used Infrequently." One by one, clear off each item on the countertop. Empty the contents of every drawer. Put your medicine chest into boxes or a garbage bag, sorting as necessary. Evaluate everything you pick up. Do you really need three bottles of half-used hairspray?

While everything is out of its storage place, wipe all the underlying surfaces clean. Then, starting with the medicine chest, replace only those items you use every day. Continue dipping into your Necessities box and placing them into drawers. Categorize each drawer according to its use: hair drawer, makeup drawer, etc.

The little plastic baskets found at discount stores are perfect as drawer dividers to keep things neat. Use two larger plastic baskets under the sink: one for cleaning items and the other for other personal toiletries you use daily, such as soap, shampoo, toothbrushes and toothpaste. Stack a few toilet rolls behind the containers. Keep the cupboard neat and only a maximum of two-thirds full.

After you have finished re-filling the shelves, there will be items remaining in the boxes. Mostly, they will be "Used Infrequently" items. Either toss these items out or pack in a labelled box ready for your move.

Focal Points: Centering your bathroom design around a focal point adds visual drama to the room. Maybe it's a marble countertop, or an imposing double vanity with a pair of mirrors, or a big soaking tub angled in the corner opposite the door. You can give the natural focal point in a room even more emphasis by using elements that naturally catch the eye. Fold or roll brightly coloured towels and place in a basket close to your focal point. Remember, red, yellow and orange are advancing colours and will draw the eye to your focal point. Position a large mirror opposite the window if possible to capture all the light. For privacy install a pretty translucent window shade or curtain that admits the light. New on the market is window wallpaper film. It is adhesive-free window film that gives ordinary windows or glass doors the look of expensive custom pieces. The film comes in a variety of designs from privacy glass to stained glass. Look for it at all good hardware or do-it-yourself stores.

If your bathroom has few redeeming features, then give your viewers a surprise memory hook by installing a crystal chandelier – as long as the bottom of the fixture is no lower than 7' from the floor. Or you can splurge on a vanity light for the mirror to create a reflective sparkle.

Colour: Always remember this. The bathroom suite fixtures, (the toilet, the sink, shower, bathtub, etc.) can be any colour – as long as they are white!

Powder Room Makeover.

That means a categorical "No" to burgundy, gold, avocado, beige or turquoise. Do not be persuaded that pastels are back in style. Stay with white. Introduce colour through tiles, flooring and accessories.

When it comes to bathroom colour, there are a few simple guidelines you need to follow to effectively get the look and feel that you want. For paint, white is the most common bathroom colour. It gives a sense of cleanliness and purity. White is ideal for small bathrooms, since it makes the room seem larger and it won't go out of style.

Sky blue paint is another popular colour, since it is believed to provide a sense of calmness and ease. The palest blue bathroom walls compliment stainless steel fixtures beautifully.

If you choose green walls, it is usually used in bathrooms in the lightest of tints to evoke peace and quiet. Green is psychologically tranquil and is most attractive during the day.

Updating cupboard handles and knobs can make a world of difference. To keep the room harmonized and calm, be careful to keep the finish of the hardware the same as the light fixtures or faucets.

If you have coloured porcelain fixtures – such as an apple green sink and toilet – and don't have the budget to change the fixtures, then work with what you have. De-emphasize the fixture colours by painting cabinetry in an analogous colour. Make it a shade darker or lighter than the fixtures. This will give you a low cost, high-impact makeover of your old fashioned bathroom. Keep the bathroom light and airy by pulling the look together with a basket of rolled up, fluffy, cream-coloured towels and accessories with a creamy white jug filled with dark brown, rough branches.

The best bathroom decorating idea is usually the simplest one. Stick to three colours at most when designing your bathroom to keep it mentally refreshing and relaxing, Take your colour inspiration from the countertop or a piece of artwork.

Lighting: There are many different bathroom lighting techniques on the market, but the one constant is the need for clear, sharp light. Vanity lighting or mirror lighting in the bathroom is crucial. This need for clear, shadowless lighting is what makes bathroom light fixtures so important. In general, fluorescent lighting is not a great choice, since it tends to make people greenish or washed out. Instead, go for soft white incandescent bulbs or CFL bulbs. Remember, the wrong bulb can make even a beautiful movie star look terrible.

Placement is the next important consideration for your bathroom light fixtures. Ideally, you should surround your face with the best light possible, minimizing shadows under the chin and eyes, while illuminating your cheeks and forehead properly.

If you have theatrical light strips with a half-dozen lamps down each side of your mirror, they should be replaced. The style is dated. This is the only point where theatre and home staging temporarily part company. Ideally, install a lamp above the mirror and sconces on either side, keeping them at least 30" (75cm) apart. This shouldn't be a problem, since the average bathroom mirror is at least this width.

Consider adding a bathroom light fixture on the ceiling and a special waterproof pot light in the shower if you have a large or a dark bathroom.

While you will want bright light to clean the bathroom and to bathe the kids, when it comes to some personal time, there can be nothing better than using a dimmer switch to soften the lighting – together with the light of a few aromatic candles carefully arranged, and the sound of your favourite relaxing music while soaking in the tub.

Space Planning: Define your space. That means identifying and reorganizing the purpose of each drawer and cupboard. Allocate the top drawer for makeup or shaving gear. Use the next drawer for your hairdryer brushes and combs. Inside the cupboard store shampoo, deodorant, hairspray, etc., in plastic dollar-store baskets. Stack toilet rolls at the back for easy retrieval. Watch for common obstacles in the bathroom that prevent you from moving around freely; the weigh-scale, an additional floor cabinet or clothes hamper. These items just occupy bathroom floor space. Pack them up or store them in the bedroom closet.

Finishing Touches: Anything from towels and shower curtains to window treatments can bring a soft touch to a hard space. Now is the time to display soft, fluffy, new towels.

Choose a shower curtain carefully. A clear curtain will add to the feeling of openness in a smaller bathroom, but a colour can help the room achieve a coordinated look.

Place facial tissues in a dispenser that matches one or more other accessories in the room, such as the toothbrush holder or lotion/soap dispenser.

Personalize décor by hanging an inexpensive framed picture or a potted plant. Low-light choices include grape ivy and a peace lily. In windowless bathrooms, display good quality silk greenery.

Set out items that offer subtle scents. Ideas include fragrant soaps, potpourri and candles, which should be changed seasonally. Use spicy fragrances in fall and winter, and floral scents in spring and summer. Add subtle, soothing, organic elements like fresh flowers. Architectural flowers like orchids and lilies are ideal. Plants/grasses, glass containers of soft-hewn pebbles or river stones are also real assets. Don't overdo the accessorizing. Make this your mantra: less is more.

The Laundry Room

The laundry room is usually a small, dreary area downstairs in the basement. It is mind-boggling that, although this room is used regularly, it is often an almost spooky area to visit. It's easy to understand why dedicated laundry rooms on the main floor of a house are coveted! If your buyer is going to have to venture into the bowels of the building to do the laundry, then you can do your best to make it an appealing, inviting place to be.

Red Flags: Replace worn hoses, fix leaks and adjust taps so they work smoothly. Get rid of stale wet rags. Remove any mould.

Clutter: Laundry rooms are notorious for collecting clutter. Clearing off shelves and installing cabinets to hide cleaning products is well worth the effort. Keep a small container handy for odds-and-ends found in pockets – before or after they spend time in the washing machine.

Focal Points: In this room, your washer and dryer will be your focal point. Make sure they are worth focusing on. In all cases, appliances should be clean and polished.

Colour: Keep the walls light coloured in the laundry room. Clean, cool colours like white and pale blue give a fresh look. Laundry appliances today come in an array of trendy colours, but you can bet that white will never go out of style.

Lighting: Install full spectrum light bulbs. Because these bulbs are similar to natural daylight, they show the true colour of your clothes. If you have the luxury of a window, make sure you treat it well with luxurious coverings. Install a motion sensor light switch that turns on the light when you walk in the laundry room and turns it off when you leave, especially appreciated when carrying an armful of laundry! This will be a small touch your buyer will carry as a memory maker.

Space Planning: If the laundry room is in the basement, make sure that the route to the area is not an obstacle course. Organize the supplies in clearly designated areas to show your buyers how efficient the space can be. Put up a shelf to store laundry detergents, softeners, stain removers, etc. If you have room, a clothes rack with hangers nearby can be added to make doing the laundry much easier.

Finishing Touches: Added niceties are a surface for folding laundry and a chair. Position a trash bin to hold discarded dryer fluff, etc. If you are in the process of washing clothes during a showing, be sure the dirty laundry is placed in a laundry basket and covered with a towel. Run a cut lemon around the inside of the laundry tub to remove stale smells.

Laundry Room Makeover.

The Basement

In an unfinished or partially finished basement, you can make a real difference with very little effort. Follow each of the Seven Steps carefully. Once you have fixed any Red Flags and conquered the Clutter, it's unbelievable what a fresh coat of paint will do. And don't forget the floor. If the floor is unfinished, paint it with concrete paint – preferably in any colour other than typical concrete grey. Install good lighting to keep the basement from feeling haunted with dark corners. Do not let inadequate lighting or stark fluorescent set the tone of the room. Make it welcoming. Hang curtains or blinds at the windows. Buyers are usually comfortable with seeing boxes stacked neatly in a basement. They know you are getting ready to move and will expect to see some sign of packing. If you have an extraordinary number of boxes, then consider putting them into storage, their very number might construe thoughts from your buyer that you are in a hurry to move and would consider accepting a lower offer. Always make sure the boxes do not block the traffic flow.

The Garage

In home staging, the garage is often overlooked. Almost everyone uses a garage as storage place for tools and garden equipment. Many people let useless and unwanted items pile up in the garage and leave their valuable car on the driveway. If you can make your garage into an attractive, well-organized area that leaves plenty of room for your car, you will make a strong impact on potential buyers who have struggled in vain to keep their own garages free of clutter. Since the garage is so often a catch-all, a clean, uncluttered area will make a very good impression. If you have managed to keep even your garage well-tended, it speaks well for your care in maintaining your property overall.

Red Flags: Check for ceiling leaks, cracks in the floor and any other neglected areas that you see. If anything is below par, get it fixed.

Clutter: Pick up items from the floor and hang them on hooks on the walls or tuck them neatly into the rafters. Tidy and clear enough away to show that you can actually park your vehicle in there.

Focal Points: The only focal point in a garage is the empty space. The purpose of a garage is to shield your car from the elements and to keep it safe. Establish that the area can do what it was intended to do.

Colour: If you have painted walls, giving them a fresh coat of white or light grey paint to make the garage clean and bright is an excellent idea. If the floor needs painting, get recommendations for a paint that's made especially for this purpose. I urge you to do your homework first and only get a recommended paint reputed to resist peeling and chipping. Some bad ones out there end up leaving your floor worse looking than when you started.

Lighting: You can never have too much light in your garage. Fluorescent lights are probably the least expensive way to get the most light in your work area. With ceilings being generally lower in garage, these lights are generally acceptable. Additional lighting can be supplied by automatic garage door openers. Just ensure that the light bulbs are to their maximum wattage and that they work!

Space Planning: Space in your garage is a no brainer. Enough space to get your car in. But also enough space to hang garden tools, and store spare tires, the lawnmower, the snow blower and any other tool that shouldn't be stored in the house.

Finishing Touches: Install hooks for hanging bikes and tools. Cabinets to store small tools are always appreciated. Reserve an area for storing recyclable products and garbage bins.

Furnishing an Empty House

Empty houses can feel as cold and unloved as the country house my husband and I left behind in England. We were unaware at the time that the consequence of leaving a house vacant can result in a lower selling price and a long stay in market limbo.

In a house with empty or partially furnished rooms, four factors make it harder to sell for the price you want. The first factor is when you have already moved; buyers tend to assume that you must be desperate to sell and will accept a much lower price. In fact, this is exactly what happened to my husband and I. Eventually we *were* desperate to sell, so we accepted a lower price.

The next factor is, if part of the furniture has been taken and only a scattering of furniture is left, it also sends the message you are desperate to sell. In this case, the buyer reasonably suspects that the family has broken up. One person has already left. And, therefore (again), the person remaining could be distracted and willing to take a lower price.

The third factor is that most people find it difficult to visualize how a room can be used when there is no furniture in it to give it scale. Leaving enough furniture in the house – even if you have to rent furniture for this purpose – can make it sell in days, instead of months. The furnishings provide a focal point and make the house feel like a home. If it is warm and inviting, it will help potential buyers make that all-important emotional connection.

The fourth factor and the most powerful disadvantage of an empty house, however, is that there are no focal points to distract attention, so every flaw is noticeable. Normal wear and tear is much more evident when there is nothing else to look at.

Help your buyers see the possibilities your house has to offer by partially furnishing and accessorizing at least the most important areas of the home, the Living/Family Room, the Dining Room, the Master Bedroom and the Bathrooms to give them an idea of scale and perspective. The minimal basic furniture and accessories for these rooms is as follows:

- **Living/Family Room**: a couch, armchair, end table, coffee table, a rug sized to fit under the furniture (if there is a hardwood floor), and a few accessories, such as a plant, toss cushions, artwork (for one or two walls) and a mirror.

- **Dining Room**: dining table, chairs, buffet or hutch, and a few accessories, such as a floor plant, table centerpiece, artwork (for one or two walls) and a mirror.
- **Master bedroom**: a headboard, bed, two side tables, two lamps, dresser, floor plant, comforter, pillows and cushions and a full-length mirror.
- **Bathrooms:**, a shower curtain, coordinating towels, fragrant soap and a candle.

The best and fastest place to find furniture – and it may not cost you a penny! – is to borrow from relatives and friends. You might also be able to purchase decent furniture from thrift shops or consignment stores. If you don't want to buy furniture, check out furniture rental outlets, or the forward-thinking furniture stores that are willing to rent furniture for a weekly or monthly fee. At these showrooms, you can select the furniture, have it delivered and picked up when the house is sold. What could be easier? Expect to pay a delivery and pickup fee, plus the weekly or monthly rental charges.

Even though no one is living in your home and it is sparsely furnished, this is not the time to save a few dollars by lowering the temperature or turning off the water. A buyer may interpret that as poor insulation or worse. It is important to keep the thermostat at a comfortable room temperature and the water turned on.

Help your buyers to picture how their furniture will fit in the space and they will start to mentally move in.

Having said all this about furnishing empty homes let me remind you that there are always exceptions to the rule. Architecturally interesting homes in immaculate shape can be shown empty without a problem. Their architectural features will serve as focal points to appeal to potential buyers' eyes.

Chapter Seven

The Top 10 Improvements Under $100

1. Buy a new welcome mat.
2. Add a potted plant in a fabulous container that coordinates with your front door colour.
3. Don't underestimate the impact of a fresh coat of paint on your front door, inside and out. It's a good idea to make sure that the paint colour complements your home. For example, if your home is mostly red brick, a glossy, jet black door would give a spectacular first impression.
4. Give your kitchen cabinets a really thorough cleaning. Then re-place all the knobs and handles. Avoid the tacky handles in the shapes of turtles and frogs other cutesy designs.
5. Install new kitchen and bathroom faucets.
6. Add a ceiling fan. In the summer months, run your ceiling fan in a counter-clockwise direction for greatest energy saving benefits. It won't replace your air conditioning, but it will make the room feel cooler by providing a breeze. Effective circulation can make you feel up to 8 degrees cooler and reduce air conditioning bills by up to 40%. In the winter months, run your ceiling fan in a clockwise direction. Warm air rises and your ceiling fan will gently re-circulate the warm air through the room without causing an unpleasantly cool breeze. This technique has been proven to lower home heating costs by as much as 10%.
7. An indoor water feature like wall fountains add moisture to the air, help block out unwanted outside sounds, such as those coming from neighbours' yards or traffic noise. It also adds a therapeutic atmosphere to the room.
8. Turn your bathroom into a spa with a new shower curtain, a basket of fluffy towels and a cluster of seven to nine votive candles.
9. Get rid of old pleated lampshades and bring your lighting into the 21st century. Shop in specialty lighting stores and ask for help with your design style.

10. Give your rooms "Wow!" factor by applying a fresh coat of paint. It will make a world of difference in the look and feel of your home. Don't use cheap paint. Purchase the best-quality paint available in a flat finish that will hide the imperfections. High gloss paint magnifies surface flaws. Semi gloss is good for door trim, baseboards and moldings.

Conclusion

As a **special free bonus (valued at $35)** for my readers, I invite you to visit www.spotlightondecor/lists.html for more Lists such as. . .

- The Top 10 Best Things to Do Before a Showing
- The Top 10 Things Most Appreciated by Viewers
- The Top 10 Worst Things to Do Before a Showing – and their Remedies.
- …and more.

Visit www.spotlightondecor.com and take a minute to subscribe to my free monthly eZine **Newsletter, filled with helpful interior decorating and home staging tips,** plus **be the first to know** about sales and special offers; simply enter your email address and hit *Go*. We value your trust and your information will be held in strictest confidence.

To help make your move even easier, my **Staging Checklist** workbook, and **Getting Ready to Move Checklist** workbook will be available soon. Their availability will be announced on my website and in my **Newsletters** – another reason to sign up for the eZine **Newsletter**

On a final note, always keep in mind that every dollar you spend on bringing your home up-to-date and back-to-life will pay off in the speed of the sale. Once my clients see what a startling difference home staging can make, many of them have wondered why they took so long to get started on these tasks. Some even wonder why they considered moving in the first place. When the home staging makes your home so appealing that you want to buy the home yourself, you know you've got a winner on your hands!

I hope you enjoyed reading this book as much I enjoyed writing it. I wish you good luck and a fast and profitable sale!

The Seductive Power
of Home Staging

A Seven-Step System for a Fast and Profitable Sale

Susan Victoria Phillips
Foreword by Paul Wilson

To purchase more copies of *The Seductive Power of Home Staging* for your clients and office, please visit www.SeductivePowerofHomeStaging.com or email order@spotlightondecor.com.

To book the author for training workshops, consulting or speaking/seminars, please contact through www.spotlightondecor.com, or email info@spotlightondecor.com, or telephone 613-271-8262.